God's Plan
For The Ages

God's Plan
For The Ages
DISPENSATIONAL TRUTH

ARTHUR D. JACKSON

WINEPRESS WP PUBLISHING

© 1998 Arthur D. Jackson

Published by:
WinePress Publishing
PO Box 1406
Mukilteo, WA 98275

Printed in the United States of America.

All rights reserved. No part of this publication may be reproduced, stored in a retrieval system, or transmitted, in any way by any means, electronic, mechanical, photocopy, recording or otherwise, without the prior permission of the publisher, except as provided by USA copyright law.

Unless otherwise noted, all Scripture is quoted from the King James Version of the Bible.

ISBN 1-57921-092-9
Library of Congress Catalog Card Number: 97-62569

Contents

Preface ix

Introduction 11

1 The Dispensations and Righteousness 25

2 The Dispensations and the Covenants 33

3 The First Dispensation 39

4 The Second Dispensation 53

5 The Third Dispensation 73

6 The Fourth Dispensation 83

7 The Fifth Dispensation 93

8   The Sixth Dispensation 117

9   The Seventh Dispensation 141

Conclusion 165
Postscript 167

Preface

This book has no other aim than to show that the living God does not operate in a haphazard or capricious manner. As seen in the Bible, He is not only a holy, moral God, but is also shown to be a very orderly being. The attempt is made herein to report to the reader what the Word of God, the Bible, clearly teaches. It is for this reason numerous quotations are used. The author is under solemn obligation not to bear false witness against the Holy Spirit, not to misrepresent Him, nor to overlay His teaching with personal opinions. As the Creator of all that exists, He had a plan, a complete plan, of all He intended to accomplish before any part of His creation was brought into being.

This book is not a cursory endeavor just to cover the subject, but is the result of many years of study and labor. After numerous years of experience in teaching these truths in Bible college, and researching the answers to hundreds of questions from inquiring students, it was thought to be time to record them for future use. It is the author's hope

Preface

that this book may be found a useful text by others laboring over these same precious truths.

This study is written to specifically avoid technical phraseology wherever and whenever possible. The author is of the persuasion there is a vast class of educated people who can read with understanding and profit in English. This study is designed for them. It is found that accurate, yes, even expert knowledge can be imparted through vernacular speech.

This presentation of God's plan for the ages is given with certain presuppositions. The Bible is considered to be the final court of appeal, and its words are regarded as infallibly inspired of God. All the facts and positions gathered in this study are taken directly from Scripture with few exceptions. There has been a conscious effort made to avoid quotations from men and from other source material. The positions arrived at in this study will stand or fall on the veracity of the written Word of God.

Though not intended to be an exhaustive examination of the subject, this study does provide a wide panorama of events that tend to clarify to believers their standing with God today. While tempered by the obvious fact that "now we see through a glass darkly," our hope is nevertheless glorious with the prospect of seeing the Lord face to face.

It is my hope that the student of the Word will find in these pages enrichment of hope and increased understanding of the divine program of God.

Arthur D. Jackson
Faculty Member
Cascade Bible College
Bellevue, WA

Introduction

A *dispensation* is a period of time in which man is tested by God in respect to his obedience to some specific revelation of the divine will. It must be a known revelation of God's will as to what He requires in the conduct of man. Thus, a dispensation consists of a period of time, referred to as an *age*, during which this specific revelation prevails as the testing of man's obedience to God.

God does not work haphazardly. Before He made the first move toward the creation of man, He had a perfect and complete plan of what He intended to do and what it was He wanted to accomplish in and through this creature. Man is a relative newcomer on this earth, as seems to be the agreement between most of the earth's sciences and scientists in general. The universe, including the earth, has been shown by the scientists to be much older than the human race. There does not seem to be any solid biblical reason to dispute that finding. Yet God saw that it was through men that He could reveal Himself to all of creation in a manner and to an extent not possible in any other way. There may have been a multitude of other plans through which He could have accomplished the same goals, but God deemed the one we are part of as being the best, so He put it into execution.

Early in this plan that God devised, sin was to become an actuality in the human race; it was here it could be dealt with and removed forever. Long before Adam and Eve were placed in the Garden of Eden, the angel Lucifer had rebelled against God, and having done so, he became Satan. It was this act of rebellion on Lucifer's part that brought sin to be an actual definite factor into the universe (Ezek. 28:14–18). It may come as a great surprise to many, but sin originated in heaven and by the highest creature God ever created. It was through this act of rebellion that sin changed from being in the realm of theory, or possibility, into that of actuality. An equally amazing truth is that it is war in heaven that is the catalyst that precipitates the end events that bring to a close the course of ungodliness and unrighteousness in all creation (cf. Rev. 12:7–12; 20:7–10).

It was this same fallen angel, Satan, who, in the guise of a serpent, deceived Eve and was the immediate cause of sin entering the human race. There are several good reasons behind God's decision to allow sin to enter the newly created human race. Foremost of these reasons being that His Son could then become a man through the incarnation, and thus be in a situation where He could pay the cost of removing sin once and for all—forever. A spiritual axiom that must be considered when delving into this problem is ". . . without the shedding of blood there is no remission [of sin]" (Heb. 9:22). The blood of the infinite Son of God had infinite value, so He could pay the price of the sum total of all the finite creatures' sin. This is the manner God chose to

Introduction

dispose of sin, which up until this time was only the theoretical opposite of holiness. He allowed sin to become an actual fact, a problem that He could correct and remove, never to be a threat again in all eternity. A second major reason for the decision was that though God Himself was not responsible for the introduction of sin into the human race, it was through sin that He would have a medium for revealing His attributes to all creation. Without the reality of sin, God had no way in which to reveal the various aspects of His character. Except in His treatment of sin, with its resulting lost and condemned race, there was no way for God to reveal His love, His mercy, His justice, His wrath, or any of the other manifold attributes that constitute His nature. The character and attributes of the great and living God are brought into an understandable focus only when in contrast to the pain, the devastation, and the hopelessness that inevitably accompany sin. It is only because of sin that the wonderful plan of salvation could be unfolded. There may be many more valid reasons for the presence of sin, but these two alone show the importance of sin in God's overall plan.

THE AGES

In the New Testament Book of Ephesians the Bible speaks of a particular dispensation, or age, that is diverse from all others. In the first chapter of that book and the tenth verse it is mentioned "that in the dispensation of the fullness of time," thereby signifying a specific age in which time, as it is known to man, will be *filled up*, complete, and will come to an abrupt end. The end of time! Men have conjectured on that possibility for generations. In our own

God's Plan for the Ages

generation there have been many cartoons, especially political cartoons, that have shown dissident characters carrying signs proclaiming the end of the world. The Bible teaches that after a time of revolt that ends in terrible judgment and destruction there will be a new heaven and a new earth (Rev. 21:1). All this activity results in the end of time as a useful tool in the measure of men's affairs.

The dispensation that is noted by this peculiar designation, "the fullness of time," is otherwise known as the millennium or the Kingdom Age. It is seen as the seventh and last of the dispensations God has recorded for the earth, following which men enter eternity. The Kingdom Age is a much-disputed period of time among men. Some even deny there ever will be a millennial kingdom with Christ personally present and reigning, despite that which the Bible clearly teaches (see Dan. 2:44; cf. Rev. 20:4). Some who teach this latter view also teach that the world today is in the millennial period and that the unseen Christ is ruling through the church. They are hard pressed to explain all the turmoil the world is experiencing instead of enjoying an extended period of peace and righteousness.

The letter to the Ephesians has a number of other references to the different ages, and these go a long way in clarifying this contentious subject. It speaks of "the ages to come" (Eph. 2:7), of "the age of grace" (Eph. 3:2), and of "other ages" (Eph. 3:5). It then uses the term "throughout all ages" (Eph. 3:1). Paul, while writing to the saints in Colosse, referred to things that were "hidden from past ages" (Col. 1:26). Christ Himself verified the existence of the different ages, when He spoke concerning the subject of sinning against the Holy Spirit, by using these words, " . . . it

Introduction

would not be forgiven in this age, nor in the age to come" (Matt. 12:32).

The Greek word used in these references is *aion* and should be and is translated to the English word *ages* in the Authorized Version. The *American Heritage Dictionary* gives the meaning of *aion* as "perpetuity" or "lasting for an indefinitely long duration." To a man of the New Testament period, a dispensation lasting between four and sixteen centuries is certainly an *aion*.

That the sovereign God had a preconceived plan for the entire creation including man is everywhere apparent in Scripture. His plan was complete to the smallest detail before any part of it was put into execution. That His program included the installation of the succession of ages is disclosed in many passages of the Bible, of which two will be looked into in some detail.

> God, who at *different* times and in *different* manners spoke in times past unto the fathers by the prophets, hath in these last days spoken unto us by His Son, whom He hath appointed heir of all things, by whom also He made the worlds. (Heb. 1:1–2, italics added)

A controversial rendering in the Authorized Version of the Greek word *aion* into the English word *worlds* has caused considerable confusion in understanding this important passage. Most scholars, especially creationists, all believed that the world came into being by an act of God. However, there was deep division among them upon the thought of the various ages being proposed as a cogent part of the creative act. It was decided that using the word *world* would be a safe alternative when translating this part of the Scripture, even though it would prove to be very inconsistent with treatment elsewhere. When verse two is translated and read rightly it would be seen to say, "by whom also He made the ages." To translate it thus would place the emphasis of this entire section of Scripture on the truth that, at different times and using different methods, God communicated with man concerning different phases of His plan. He did not reveal the total plan all at once but was progressive in His revelation, each part building upon and expanding on that which went before.

The second passage to be examined was written by that highly educated man, Doctor Luke; for he wrote the words, "Known unto God are all His works from the beginning of the aion [ages]" (Acts 15:18). Again, this passage emphasizes the fact that, from the beginning, God had an entire plan. This was no aimless venture He set in motion. The word *works* is seen to be in the plural. Thus, it may be deduced that while God settled on a single complete plan, that plan had many individual parts; nevertheless, all parts fit precisely together to make a perfect whole. It is in the light of these truths and seen from this advantageous position that it may be understood with clarity why it was necessary for God to instruct men to,

> Study to show thyself approved unto God, a workman that needeth not to be ashamed, rightly dividing the word of truth. (2 Tim. 2:15)

THINGS SHARED BETWEEN FRIENDS

> Henceforth I call you not servants; for the servant knoweth not what his lord doeth: but I have called you

Introduction

friends; for all things that I have heard of my Father I have made known unto you. (John 15:15)

The Lord has revealed many new truths to the individuals who make up the true Church, His Bride. These new things all fall under the subject of New Testament mysteries, which makes a most fascinating study for the serious student of the Word. The word *mystery* occurs twenty-seven times in the Authorized Version of the New Testament. It is a translation of the Greek word *musterion,* a derivative of *muo,* which in turn is defined to mean to *shut the mouth* or more simply *silence.* A common word used today that has the same root source is the word *mustache*—hair on the upper lip. The Greek word *mystax* (upper lip) and also the word *mastax,* translated "mouth or jaw", are both of this same family. It follows along very smoothly then to understand that when we eat a meal, we masticate our food before swallowing. In the light of the foregoing truth, it can be concluded that the word *mystery* as used in the New Testament would literally mean "a closed-mouth silence."

The modern dictionary meaning of the word *mystery* is twofold: (1) something which is unintelligible, incomprehensive, baffling, or uncanny; and (2) something that may be known but only by the initiated. In contrast, the ancient meaning is connected with the ancient cults of Babylon and of Rome, and it follows the course of the second meaning as listed above. The heathen religious ceremonies practiced by these cults consisted of rites considered sacred and observed in strictest secrecy. Those who were initiated into the order were known as the *perfected* and were then exposed to these rites.

The New Testament and biblical definition of a mystery is best seen in the apostle Paul's letter to the Church in Ephesus when he wrote,

> That which in other ages was *not made known* unto the sons of men, as it is *now revealed* unto his holy apostles and prophets by the Spirit. (Eph. 3:5, italics added)

This is not an isolated text but is very much reinforced by several other Scriptures, such as the one found in the last chapter of the letter to the church at Rome.

> Now to him that is of power to establish you according to my gospel, and the preaching of Jesus Christ, according to the revelation of the *mystery*, which was *kept secret* since the world began, but *now* is made manifest, and by the scriptures of the prophets according to the commandment of the everlasting God, made known to all nations for the obedience of faith. (Rom.16:25–26, italics added)

God, in the Scriptures, repeats this truth the third time for even greater emphasis when He has Paul explain in the letter to the Colossians,

> Even the *mystery* which has been *hidden* from ages and from generations, but *now* is made manifest to his saints, to whom God would make known what is the riches of the glory of this *mystery* among the Gentiles, which is Christ in you, the hope of glory. (Col. 1:26–27, italics added)

An old cliché that made the rounds many years ago said, "We should make much of that which God makes much

Introduction

of." Such a cliché seems very proper and fitting in this particular instance. When God repeats a truth three times there has to be a reason for it—a very good reason.

We conclude then that, as used in the New Testament, the *mysteries* embody those truths that, in the ages prior to the Pentecost recorded in Acts 2, were kept in silence but are *now*—in this the *Church Age*—made the common property of all believers. They are not special truths for an elite group, but every believer is privileged to understand and possess the knowledge of these mysteries. In fact, each and every believer has a definite responsibility before God to both know and teach these truths. For God's Word discloses,

> Let a man so account of us, as of the ministers of Christ, and stewards of the mysteries of God. Moreover, it is required in stewards, that a man be found faithful. (1 Cor. 4:1–2)

The word *stewards* as used in these verses is very intriguing and worthy of some research. The use of such easily available sources as encyclopedias, dictionaries, concordances, etc. can be of extensive value in this type of study to give depth and insight to words used in the Scriptures. *Strong's Exhaustive Concordance* gives the word *stewards* as the translation of the Greek word *oikonomia*; the apostle Paul used that word here in 1 Corinthians. Further study shows this same Greek word *oikonomia* occurs three times in Luke 16, and there each time it is rendered *stewardship* (Luke 16:2, 3, 4). On four other occasions in the New Testament this word is translated *dispensation* (1 Cor. 9:17; Eph. 1:10, 3:2; Col. 1:25). It is easy indeed to see that the English word *economy*, which means *to manage*, is derived from this Greek word. The *Reader's Digest Great Encyclopedic Dictionary* defines *economy* as "frugal management of money, materials, resources, and the like; freedom from extravagance; thrift."

It takes no great imagination to recognize the word *dispense* as the core of the larger word *dispensation*. Again, using the dictionary, *dispense* means "to give or deal out in portions; to distribute; to administer, as laws." The modern English word *stewardship* is derived from the old German *stigweard,* which has a literal translation as *house warden*. The dictionary explains it this way: "An officer or employee in a large family, estate, etc. to manage the domestic concerns, supervise servants, collect rents, keep accounts, etc. The steward would be an administrator, supervisor, manager in a closed economy."

It is in this manner that the importance and magnitude of what the apostle Paul has written in 1 Cor. 4:1–2, concerning every believer being a steward or having stewardship, dawns upon the reader. Each Christian has a responsibility not only to read and know the different New Testament mysteries but to be able to teach (distribute) them to others.

The Mystery Age

The Church Age is best known by its more popular name, the Age of Grace. A third name, and perhaps the most appropriate, is the Mystery Age—and will be the one used in this study. This Mystery Age began on the day of Pentecost (Acts 2) and will continue until the day when the Church is raptured (caught up) to meet the Lord in the air. The Church itself is a New Testament mystery since it is entirely unknown and unrevealed in Old Testament scrip-

Introduction

tures. The body of the Old Testament does not give even a single hint of the New Testament Church, which is collectively made up of regenerated individuals cleansed, purified, declared by God to be righteous, and thus blameless before Him. It is the Church, the body of which Christ is the head, that is the basic theme around which all the other mysteries revolve. The individual mysteries lead toward the Church, or surround it in a revealing fashion, and collectively they expose this culminating work of God to the minds and understanding of inquiring men who desire to know of God and His plans for this age. The New Testament mysteries reveal the Church for what it is—its composition, its purpose, its character, its history, its relationship to Christ, and much other pertinent data. All that may be known of the true Church, the corporate body of Christ, is found in the messages that the New Testament mysteries provide. All of the New Testament mysteries are very much applicable in this age in which we now live.

Following are listed fifteen New Testament mysteries in the order they occur in the Scripture. It may be noted the first two are found to be in the Gospels and the last two are located in the Book of Revelation, recorded by the apostle John. All the rest of the recorded mysteries lie between these two pairs and are given to us through the ministry of the apostle Paul.

The first two mysteries actually locate the Church in reference to other parts of God's overall program. The Church will be seen as comprising a part of both the kingdom of Heaven and the kingdom of God but having some important differences when compared with each. The Church is composed only of those born-again members of all the generations of this present mystery age, generations both past and present. With the Church Age now approaching its 2,000-year mark, and allowing three generations to the century, the believers of today make up about the sixtieth generation of that body. Because of their born-again experience they are referred to as the *good seed* or as *wheat*. In comparison, the kingdom of Heaven is concerned only with the generation living at any given moment of time, and it embraces both wheat and tares. There is a vast difference—a life-and-death difference—between those who truly possess Christ as their Savior and those who merely profess to know Him. For this reason the kingdom of Heaven in any given generation is seen to be much larger than the true Church of the same period of time. The Church is seen also to be part of the kingdom of God, but this kingdom is far greater in scope than the Church. The kingdom of God is essentially a spiritual kingdom, and it contains all creatures of all time who are willing subjects of God's rule. Thus the kingdom of God includes the holy angels, the Old Testament saints, the Church, and will include the Tribulation saints as well as the future kingdom saints, etc.

It is to be concluded that every true believer of this Mystery Age is a member of three different God-ordained economies: first, as a born-again believer he is a member of the Church—the corporate body, of which Christ is the head. Second, he is a member of the kingdom of Heaven in its mystery form—restricted to those living and present here on earth. And third, he is a member of the spiritual and eternal kingdom of God. The literal kingdom of Heaven, known as the *millennial kingdom*, has been postponed until the return of its King after the Mystery Age is complete. God's main thrust and purpose in this present age is the "calling out" of the Church. This Church is named the Bride

Introduction

of Christ, and she is the one who will sit by His side and rule with Him during all of the next age, which is known as the *millennium*—the literal kingdom of Heaven. Ruling with Christ simply means each Christian will be the Lord's representative and will exercise full authority in the community in which he or she resides. Zion, in Jerusalem, will be the central seat of power; for that is where Jesus Himself will rule.

The final two mysteries, both found in the Book of Revelation, give the course and the history of the true Church throughout this age, which is then followed by the course and destruction of the false church that remains on earth after the true Church is removed. The remaining eleven mysteries, which are boxed between these two pair, are taken from the Epistles and are from the pen of the apostle Paul. According to Ephesians 3 we are told he received them by direct revelation from God.

> How that by revelation he made known unto me the mystery . . . by which, when you read, you may understand my knowledge in the mystery of Christ. (Eph.3:3–4)

1. The Mysteries of the Kingdom of Heaven — Matt. 13
2. The Mysteries of the Kingdom of God — Mark 4:11; Luke 8:10
3. The Mystery of Israel's Blindness — Rom. 11:25
4. The Mystery of the Wisdom of God — 1 Cor. 2:7; Col. 2:2
5. The Mystery of the Change (before the Rapture) — 1 Cor. 15:51
6. The Mystery of His Will — Eph. 1:9

7. The Mystery of Christ (the Church) — Eph. 3:3–9
8. The Mystery of the Church (the Bride) — Eph. 5:32
9. The Mystery of the Gospel — Eph. 6:19
10. The Mystery of the Inliving Christ — Col. 1:26
11. The Mystery of Iniquity — 2 Thess. 2:7
12. The Mystery of Faith — 1 Tim. 3:9
13. The Mystery of Godliness — 1 Tim. 3:16
14. The Mystery of the Seven Stars — Rev. 1:20
15. Mystery Babylon — Rev. 17:5–7

These mysteries comprise the bulk of Church truth and are separate from, and complementary to, Old Testament teaching. In each case the New Testament use of the word *mystery* indicates a new work of God that was hitherto unrevealed, totally unknown and untaught in the Old Testament.

Chapter 1

The Dispensations and Righteousness

One may ask, Why the dispensations? In the beginning God created man in a state of innocence, which means man had no knowledge of good or evil. In this state man was not tainted by sin, evil, or guilt. While man was created innocent, he was not created righteous. Righteousness is defined as doing that which is right; it only comes as a result of right action. God could not create righteousness, but He could create conditions that would be a test to, if passed correctly, produce righteousness. The one characteristic that God is always seeking for and desires to find in His creature man is righteousness. As the Creator, God knew the creature was incapable of producing or even maintaining a righteousness acceptable to His standards. His problem was to convince man of this fact. The way He chose to accomplish this difficult task was to introduce a series of tests and expose man to them age by age. God wants the creature to understand that no matter what the conditions or the circumstances may be, he (the creature) in his own attempts will *always* fall short of the perfection that God demands and will accept. Because God is perfect He will accept nothing less than perfection in the creature's approach to Him. It is for this reason that when a man comes before God for acceptance he must come clothed in God's own righteousness; nothing else will do.

Righteousness in its pure form is a precious, priceless commodity. The Psalmist attests to this truth when he says, "for the righteous Lord loveth righteousness." In contrast to this impressive statement, the Lord has said that all the righteousness that man is capable of producing has no more value than a filthy detestable rag (Isa. 64:6). Righteousness must be of the everlasting variety or nature before God will take note of it. This is exactly what the Old Testament declares when it says that one of the names that He has claimed for His own is "the Lord our Righteousness" (Jer. 23:5–6). The New Testament agrees with this truth totally concerning all who accept Jesus as Savior by saying, "we might be made the righteousness of God in Him" (2 Cor. 5:21).

The conclusion to be drawn is that true righteousness is closely related to the character of God Himself. There is an inextricable tie between the nature of God and His actions. The Psalmist said, "Thy righteousness is an everlasting righteousness" (Ps.119:142). Everything that is of an everlasting nature must of necessity originate from God.

The writers of the Psalms have much to say about God and His attribute of righteousness. They begin by saying ". . . the righteous Lord loves righteousness" (11:7); "He loves righteousness and hates wickedness" (45:7); His "right hand is full of righteousness" (48:10); He leads His followers in "paths of righteousness" (23:3); and then they assert that the very "heavens shall declare His righteousness" (50:6). Even when there is no course left to Him but that of wrath and anger, the Psalmist says, "He shall judge the world in righteousness" (9:8).

To all this is added the witness of the New Testament writers who say "the heart of man believes unto righteousness" (Rom.10:10). This is speaking of no less than faith in God and in His Word. The regenerated man is to follow after righteousness, godliness, faith (1 Tim. 6:11), and peace (2 Tim. 2:2). The apostle John has written ". . . every one that does [practices] righteousness is born of God" (1 John 2:29), and then goes on to say "he that practices righteousness is righteous" (3:7). The reverse is equally true: "whosoever does not [practice] righteousness is not of God" (3:10). To top it all off, the apostle Paul assures each believer that part of the hope that is set before us now is that a crown of righteousness is laid up for each of us and will be given in that future time when we shall see Him (2 Tim. 4:8).

The holiness and the righteousness of God are the two attributes that are the buttresses, the rock-solid foundation, within which all the rest of the character of God is contained and operates. These two are infinite, without measure in their scope, and are largely responsible for the awesome majesty of His presence. It is only when men see God in the light of these two attributes that they find themselves in a mental location that is but a short step from salvation. To compare one's sinful self to the beauty of His holiness and sinless perfection is to see the hopelessness of one's position and the utter need for help (salvation) from outside one's own abilities.

The irony of the situation is that these are the same two characteristics that God is looking for and desires to find in men. This truth is clearly demonstrated in the illustration of the Old Testament character of Abraham, of whom the Scripture record says, "Abraham believed God, and it was counted unto him for righteousness" (Rom. 4:3). In this quoted passage it does not say that Abraham became righteous, but that through obedience to God's word he was justified, which means he was declared to be righteous on the grounds of another individual's (Christ) work. As Abraham believed God and has become the prime example for all generations to follow, even so all men today are being tested for the identical purpose. The subject of the test may change from dispensation to dispensation, but the purpose never does. This is why the message for today is very short and very direct. The New Testament tells the men of this generation, "Believe on the Lord Jesus Christ, and thou shalt be saved."

Why the dispensations? Men have debated over this issue for centuries. In fact the subject of dispensationalism has been the source of much of the splintering and fragmenting that has occurred in the Christian Church during the past generations. We have been instructed to "rightly divide the word of truth" but never to divide or splinter the Church. Satan has chosen this subject as one of several that are very adaptable to his program of bringing in confusion and chaos—and through this process, division. Men are creatures prone to follow other men who appear to be strong leaders. Many men have written commentaries expressing their ideas and beliefs on the subject of the dispensations, and each in turn has found a following willing to go along with his ideas. This is an age-old trick of our archenemy, Satan, for he likes nothing more than to get God's people to follow the teaching of men rather than the immutable Word of God, the Bible. The apostle Paul, when confronted by this very problem during the infancy of the Church, wrote to the local assembly in Corinth saying:

> Now this I say, that every one of you saith, I am of Paul; or I, of Apollos; or I, of Cephas; or I, of Christ. Is Christ divided? Was Paul crucified for you? Or were ye baptized in the name of Paul? (1 Cor.1:12–13)

In this study the aim is to let the Bible speak for itself. In His master plan, God decreed there would be seven dispensations. God could foresee that men would push the claim that if put under the right set of circumstances he (man) could or would meet all God's stringent demands to be declared righteous. To prove to the race that their thinking was wrong, God determined to place men in seven different conditions and allow them to fail in each as they tried in their own strength to attain to His standards. The sovereign God knew, through His attribute of omniscience, that seven ages or dispensations would cover the entire range of circumstances to befall the human race. God has predicted the outcome of this series of tests many times and in different ways, for the Scripture says, "There is none righteous, no, not one," and, "There is none that doeth good, no, not one." (Rom.3:10, 12). The Old Testament speaks equally of man's inability, for it says, "There is a way which seemeth right unto man, but the end thereof are the ways of death" (Prov. 14:12). As the Creator, God knew that the creature could not reach the perfection of His standard, and He said through the prophet Isaiah,

> For my thoughts are not your thoughts, neither are your ways my ways, sayeth the LORD. For as the heavens

are higher than the earth, so are my ways higher than your ways, and my thoughts than your thoughts." (Isa. 55:8–9)

The seven ages have been given names that are able to keep the different ages separate and distinct. The names of the seven dispensations that are generally recognized by dispensationalists are:

1. Innocence
2. Conscience
3. Human government
4. Promise
5. Law
6. Grace/Church
7. Kingdom

Most authors in the late twentieth century, when writing on the subject of the dispensations, whether they are pro or con, limit their study to the final three ages and either overlook or else completely ignore the first four of the total seven. They do this to the hurt and injury of their constituents, and consequently to the whole church, because this leaves a large gap in the body of truth. The readers of such limited information can only come away with a lopsided understanding of the subject being studied. The Word says, "*All* scripture is given by inspiration of God and is profitable . . . for instruction in righteousness" (2 Tim. 3:16, italics added). Furthermore, the Lord said, ". . . ye shall know the truth and the truth shall make you free" (John 8:32).

Within the teachings of the final three ages is contained a separate and individual way of life. This is where the admonition of Scripture applies when it says of the believer that he should not be ashamed, but rather he should rightly divide the Word; that is, he should keep the lines of truth separate and unmixed (2 Tim. 2:15). When lines of truth from one way of life are intermixed with lines of truth from another way, then doubt and confusion reign. It is by recognition of the various ages, and the specific test that is employed during any one of them, that a clear picture of God's plan and His purpose for man begins to emerge. The beginning of all seven of the dispensations finds man (or men) in close fellowship with God. During the course of each age, man fails in his responsibility before God, and each dispensation ends in judgment as sin brings on its inevitable result.

It is the intent of this study to examine each of the seven ages in all the light that is available. In order to succeed, the same format will be used for each separate age as far as possible. The format to be used is one that has evolved through many classes on the subject with students in Bible school or in adult Bible classes. This format answers many of the questions that arose during class sessions.

THE OUTLINE TO BE USED

The Number and the Name of the Dispensation
    I. The time (using Usher's chronology)
        A. The state of man at the beginning of the dispensation
        B. Man's responsibility during the dispensation
            1. Usually discovered in a covenant
   II. The length of the dispensation
  III. The close of the dispensation
        A. The failure of man

  B. The activity of Satan
  C. The judgment that closes the dispensation
IV. The direct dealing of God

Chapter 2

The Dispensations and the Covenants

The Bible reveals the Lord is testing man through a series of seven consecutive ages or time periods. This testing, in most instances, is done in conjunction with a series of covenants that He makes with men. The Bible further reveals there are eight of these covenants that fit within the framework of the seven ages, otherwise known as dispensations. The first four dispensations each have a single covenant apiece detailing the responsibilities God expects man to fulfill during the tenure of that covenant. The fifth dispensation has three different but complementary covenants. The sixth age has no covenant at all. And the seventh, yet future, has the promise of a new covenant, which God will announce at the proper time (see Jer. 31:31–33; Heb. 8:8).

The American Heritage Dictionary defines a covenant as: "A binding agreement made by two or more parties; a compact; contract. Theol. God's promises to man, as recorded in Old and New Testaments." The first statement of this definition is a good explanation of a *conditional* covenant, where both parties are subject to predetermined provisos. The second, or theological, definition covers an unconditional covenant in which only one party (God) is subject to the provisions subscribed. In an unconditional covenant God says, "I will do such and so." His will and actions are not dependent upon any reciprocal action on the part of men. Of the eight biblical covenants recorded, seven are unconditional and only one is found to be conditional. This single conditional covenant—the fifth in the series and referred to as the Mosaic covenant—is one in which God said to Israel, "*If* you will do so and so, then I will do this in return" (see Exod.19:5).

The first three of these binding covenants were made between God and the whole human race. The men living at the time each covenant was proposed were men acting as representatives for the race, and they agreed to abide by all the stipulations set forth. All men of all time live and act under the provisions and conditions determined in these three compacts. At no time in human history has any of these covenants been rescinded. The final five covenants have all been made by the Lord with the nation of Israel, or perhaps it would be better said, with the Jewish people. As with the first three covenants, those made with the Jewish people have never been annulled, and so remain in effect at this time. The last covenant has not yet become an actuality, but it has been promised by the Lord, and so it is as sure as His word.

It was mentioned in passing that no covenant was associated with the sixth dispensation, the Church Age. There is no covenant made with the Church. It is important to realize there was no second party involved when Jesus, the Christ, proclaimed His intent to build the Church. The Lord simply said, "I will build My church . . ." (Matt.16:18). The Church is not a covenanted body; it did not begin nor does it continue to exist and grow as the result of an agreement. Rather, the Church is a New Testament creation. It took the sacrificial death of Jesus and the regenerating work of the Holy Spirit to bring the Church into existence. The Bible says,

> For where a testament is, must also of necessity be the death of the testator. For a testament is of force after men are dead; otherwise it is of no strength at all while the testator liveth. (Heb. 9:16–17)

From this passage of Scripture it may be easily recognized how the title of the New Testament Church was derived. The death of the testator is an absolute must to make a testament effective. While He was living and ministering to the people, Jesus, in a moment of prophesy said, ". . . I will build my church . . ." (Matt. 16:18). The fulfillment of that utterance was not begun until after His death and resurrection. Of the eight covenants spoken of in the Old Testament, not one is associated with the death of one of its two-or-more participants, so they could not possibly be classified as testaments. There are many preachers and teachers today who claim the words *covenant* and *testament* are interchangeable and synonymous. This even extends to some of the translations of the Bible that are so popular. Such a claim is in error and can only lead to confusion. Luke 22:20 says, "This cup is the new testament in my blood, which is shed for you." This is a correct rendering of the truth being conveyed to the reader of this passage. Even so, there is a marginal note directed to this verse which says, "or covenant," and it immediately raises doubt and becomes the source of unneeded confusion. What is true of this quote from Luke is also true of the parallel passages in Mark 14:24 and in Matthew 26:28.

There is a statement in the *Student Edition of the Dictionary of the Bible* by Philip Schaff, D.D. LL.D., published in 1880, that reads as follows, "The titles Old and New Testaments arose from the inaccurate rendering of the word covenant by *testamentum* in the Latin Vulgate." If this statement be true then the translators, at this point, committed a real disservice that the English-speaking believers have paid dearly for ever since. Contrary to the teaching of some, the words *testament* and *covenant* are not synonyms and, therefore, are not interchangeable.

The five past ages have one thing in common: Men in each age have had their responsibilities toward God spelled out for them in a bond or covenant that He had clearly made with them. That both parties were fully aware of the responsibilities is apparent, in that God has held men accountable when they failed to meet their obligations, and judgment soon followed each failure.

The sixth age, which is the present, is different from all other ages in that this is the age that God chose to call out the Church, the Bride, for His Son. This is an arbitrary and sovereign choice, but God is free to act in this manner. God did not covenant or make an agreement with any second party concerning the building of His Church. The decision was entirely His, and His alone.

Jesus, in His first work on earth, made all the necessary preparations for the Church. Not only did He promise there would be a Church (Matt. 16:18), but He further promised to send the Holy Spirit, the chief architect and builder (John 14:16–17; 16:7). All that the New Testament has to say concerning the Church comes as a revelation through the ministry of the Spirit of Christ. The New Testament is made through Christ, sealed by His blood, and it secures to everyone who believes the blessings of salvation and eternal life. The New Testament required the death of Christ before it could become effective. The gospel of salvation says,

> Christ died for our sins . . . that he was buried, and that he arose again. . . .(1 Cor. 15:1–4)

Chapter 3

The First Dispensation

The first dispensation is referred to as the Age of Innocence. The time of this dispensation was from the moment of the creation of Adam until the time of his disobedience of the specific instructions from God. This rebellion by Adam has come to be known as the *Fall*—the fall from a warm fellowship with God to a condition of estrangement, enmity, and death. Adam was created in a state of innocence, but not that of righteousness. Righteousness is only attained as the result of *doing* right. Having been created a being in a condition of innocence, Adam had no perception of that which was right or wrong, good or evil. Wanting to find righteousness in the first couple of humans, as He does in all humans, God put them to a very simple test. They were commanded to abstain from eating the fruit of one tree in the garden. All the trees, with the one exception, were for their pleasure.

There was another matter, a second circumstance, that Adam in his state of innocence didn't know. Lucifer, the highest of the angels—and thus the highest of all created beings—had already openly rebelled against God and had become Satan. During this time, while God was giving instruction to Adam, sin already existed in creation but was not yet in the human race. Lucifer, hostile against God, sought to destroy all that God had created and pronounced as good. It was just a short while before he subtly approached Eve and then deceitfully enticed her to eat fruit of the forbidden tree; in doing so, she broke God's command.

While studying the state of man at his creation, it is found that he was in a state of innocence; and, as such, he was in full, unbroken communion and fellowship with his Creator. The two, God and man, walked and talked together, and it was a time of complete bliss. A wise man many years later put into expression the relationship that exists between two such friends. He said, "Can two walk together, except they be agreed?" (Amos 3:3). Man's full responsibility toward his Maker in this first dispensation can be seen in the seven points of what is now known as the Edenic Covenant.

The Edenic Covenant

This covenant was made between God and the human race, even though the race at this time consisted of but two members. The seven points of this covenant are located in the Book of Genesis in 1:28 and 2:15–17. They are:

1. Be fruitful, multiply and fill the earth
2. Subdue the earth for human uses
3. Have dominion over the entire animal creation
4. Eat only herbs and fruits. (They were to be vegetarians)
5. Till the soil and keep the garden

The First Dispensation

6. Abstain from eating the fruit of one tree
7. The penalty for disobedience: death

These seven points cover the total responsibility given by God to the people of the first dispensation; nothing was to be added and nothing detracted. If they had lived up to the demands of this simple covenant, they would have lived forever in Eden and have been blessed of God.

In reality, the dispensation was short—very short. To put an actual figure of years to the length of this first age of man would be sheer guesswork. What is known is that it ended before the birth of the first child, believed to be Cain. The Bible says that Adam was only 130 years old at the birth of Seth (Gen. 5:3). Seth may have been the third child born to Eve, although the probability is that there were a number of other children, both boys and girls, who preceded him. This would help in answering the question concerning Cain's wife; she may have been a sister.

The close of the dispensation came at the failure of man. This is just the first of seven failures, for each age ends the same way: with man committing error, exposing the irresponsibility of the creature. Man, without help from a source outside himself, is simply unable to meet the high standards of a holy, sovereign God. Eve listened to the tempter and succumbed to his entreaty. Adam, on the other hand, saw what his wife had done, and in an act of love toward her, willingly took of the forbidden fruit and joined her in this rebellious escapade. This act of love on Adam's part was misplaced love, for surely his love for God should have had a much higher priority than his love for a fellow creature, even his wife.

Satan's activity will now be duly noted. As is so often the case, Satan's attack, or his ruse, came through a third party. This is a highly-effective ploy, one he uses frequently. Satan seldom attacks openly, but he comes disguised or concealed in order to deceive. Men "love darkness rather than light because their deeds are evil" (John 3:19). What is stated of men is even more true of Satan. While still in junior high school, my whole class was intensely intrigued when the mathematics teacher said proving "one-half equals one" was an elementary procedure. Having gained everyone's attention, he then said, "A half-truth equals one lie." For a moment the class sat stunned, with not a word or a sound as the truth sunk in.

This is precisely the tactic Satan used when he approached Eve on that fateful occasion. What he told her was the truth—but only half the truth. This is far different than saying it was only half true. Satan, through his emissary the serpent, said to her, "God knows that in the day you eat from it your eyes will be opened, and you will be like God, knowing good and evil" (Gen. 3:5). That statement from Satan is true. What Satan did not say, however, was of equal importance to Eve: that while knowing good and evil, she lacked the moral or spiritual strength within herself to do the right and turn away from wrong. All Eve could see for the moment was that God was withholding something good from her.

In uncovering all of Satan's deceit, it is discovered he cleverly concealed a lie in his discussion with Eve. He clearly contradicted God's Word when he told her, "You surely shall not die" (Gen. 3:5). Thus, it is seen that he adroitly mixed truth, half-truth, and falsehood in one conversation. This is the account of the first meeting between a human and the enemy, Satan; and it points up the necessity of knowing the truth, God's Word, and standing by it. There is no other way to combat spiritual error, with any expectation of coming away victorious, than by being fully acquainted with the Bible and, as much as one is able, to have memorized the Word. The Bible says, "Resist the devil and he will flee from you" (James 4:7). The most effective way of doing this is to be able to quote Scripture.

The Judgment Following Failure

It is well to take a good long and profound inspection of the judgment that resulted from the failure that occurred during the test that ended the first of the series of ages. The details of this judgment are recorded in Genesis 3:14–19, 24. The first segment of this judgment focused on the serpent, who was cursed and humbled (Gen. 3:14). We have no idea of the state of the serpent prior to its being cursed. It may have been a creature that walked upright. Certainly Eve showed no fear of its presence. Most likely it was a beautiful creature. Even today it shows the residual beauty of what it once was. Many serpents are very colorful. Some have very intricate designs in their skins, and most all show a supple, sinuous grace in movement that is suggestive of the place they once held. Neither the presence of the serpent nor its ability to communicate with her seemed to subdue Eve to any degree. Possibly it was natural that the most beautiful creature ever created, Lucifer (Ezek. 28:12–15), should choose one of the most beautiful creatures on earth to be his tool in his nefarious scheme.

Since the time of the serpent being cursed, there has been a general abhorrence and fear of this creature by all mankind. This fear seems to apply to the entire family of serpents, both the poisonous and the nonpoisonous alike. Satan, as the antitype, has been scripturally termed "that old serpent" (Rev. 12:9, 20:2), and he comes under this same curse also. God has declared that enmity would exist between the serpent and the children of men. Jesus, as the Son of man, destroyed the power of Satan when He died on the cross, was buried, and then arose again in victory over death and sin in fulfillment of the prophecy given in Genesis 3:15. This seemed like a total victory for Satan, but the resurrection of Jesus the Lord was the destruction of Satan's power and the forecast of his doom.

The core of the next segment of the judgment pronounced applies to the woman. God said that the woman (or women) would suffer pain and travail while giving birth. Suffering, pain, sickness, and death are all the direct result of sin. Because Eve took the lead part in disobeying God's instructions, He pronounced this particularly perilous experience to be the price she was to pay. Sin does not come cheaply. The passage in Genesis 3 seems to cover more than just the act of giving birth to a child, but would also include child rearing. This larger field of endeavor would encompass caring for, feeding, nursing, training, and all the other inherent duties required of the mother of a young child. Entailed among all these responsibilities there would be times of fatigue, anxiety, worry, sleeplessness, and exhaustion. For many mothers these things are an on-going series of trials as long as the mother-child relationship exists.

With the advent of the feminist movement there has been a coordinated, systematic effort to bypass much of the responsibility of being a mother. Society has fostered a need for, and then established a system of, daycare centers for preschool infants. These, along with a growing pool of

The First Dispensation

professional baby sitters, has made it easy for many mothers to pursue interests outside the home and family. It is in this manner that modern society is attempting to thwart that which God has ordained, and in so doing has become an active agent in its own destruction.

It was God's purpose that man and woman should share equally in the effects of their rebellion against Him. The next detail in the complex judgment that God pronounced at this time was that He cursed the ground (earth). In doing this He caused the requirement of great effort on the part of man to wrest an adequate food supply, where previously there had been a great source, easy to obtain for all their needs. This curse is the same one that Paul speaks of, and tells of its removal, in Romans 8:19–22. Special notice should be taken that God did not curse man, but rather cursed the ground from which man derived his livelihood. One of Satan's titles is "the god of this world." When and how he received this title is not revealed, only the future will expose this truth. It would appear that Satan was present on this earth before Adam was created. What relationship exists between Satan and the earth is not fully understood, but we do know that the Scripture says during our present age, the earth (ground) is under a curse. In summation, man's fate is sorrow, toil, sweat, and finally death—the resultant return to the earth from which he came (Gen. 3:19).

Supplementary Notes

When God formed Eve, she was made as a fit mate for Adam. She was his equal in all things, with the possible exception of physical prowess. Eve was not inferior to Adam in any appreciable way. The two were complementary to each other, and together they formed a single composite unit (Gen. 2:18).

The story of the first couple, as it is told in the opening chapters of the Bible, is a true illustration of the progress of temptation as it leads to sin. Satan has an assortment of tricks that has varied little in his sordid career. That which worked well for him against our early forebears works equally well today. This story in Genesis tells of the time and the event when sin first entered the human race. It rightly closes the door on the excuses men fabricate for their penchant for sinning. Men would like to blame their environment for their sin, but for Adam the environment was perfect. Other men put their fingers on heredity as the cause, but again looking at the illustration of Adam and Eve, who had no parents, heredity couldn't have been a factor.

Satan's precedent-setting devices have changed very little with the passage of time. In the past, temptation came to Eve well disguised. Satan did not approach Eve directly, but rather he came to her through the medium of a third party. The contact was made through a creature over whom Adam and Eve were to have dominion. Satan then took a clear-cut command of God and turned it into a topic for debate. It may come as a surprise, but the first recorded inquiry in Scripture was a question as to the veracity of the Word of God (Gen. 3:1). The creature said, "Yea, has God said . . . ?"

In the vernacular of today, "Did God really say that?" Or it may be worded slightly differently such as, "Did God really mean that?" This method worked so well that Satan has used it many times in the intervening years. Today it is one of his most successful tools.

The First Dispensation

The question asked repeatedly by men while reading the Bible is, "Is this really what God meant to say?" When such a question is asked, the inquirer is usually in trouble as deep as that in which Eve found herself. It has been well stated, "If God didn't mean what He said, then who can say what He did mean?" The twentieth-century Church is a badly fractured and greatly weakened entity because of the effectiveness of this ruse—which is just one of the many ploys that Satan has in his arsenal. In asking this question, Satan's motive was to raise doubt in Eve's mind concerning God's goodness. He planted the seed that caused her to believe God was withholding something good from her. Inadvertently, Satan provided Eve with the reason why God thought it necessary to give the command that He did.

At this point the temptation of Eve was over. Her mind was now concentrating on the forbidden. She recognized the fruit was good to look at, next she found it was of good taste and good for food, and lastly she became convinced it was desirable to make her wise (Gen. 3:6). These three steps correspond exactly with the word given in 1 John 2:16, which says that from the world come the three sources of temptation: the lust of the eye, the lust of the flesh, and the pride of life. Furthermore, the Hebrew word translated *desirable* in the sixth verse is also found in the tenth commandment, which says "thou shalt not covet."

The advent of sin into the human race caused God to declare an entirely new order of things pertaining to man and his environment. Much has been changed. Shame has taken the place of innocence, fear has replaced fellowship, painful toil has supplanted dominion, and death reigns over all. The woman now enters a new relationship with man—she will be subject to him (Gen. 3:16). This verse says in part, ". . . thy desire shall be to thy husband," and the word *desire* seems to convey the idea of prompting to sin. It is as if God is saying, "You tried to lead—you shall be dominated."

Among unsaved, unregenerate people this has led to harsh, cruel, exploitative treatment of women by men. In some countries of the world, women and girls are treated as if they are mere possessions with little intrinsic value. Their treatment is like that given to slaves, and the major concern of the male centers around the amount of usefulness that can be derived from them. It is only the presence of the Holy Spirit that removes the heartless male domination so characteristic of the world. The Christian Church, with its biblical teaching, has been a major supporter of women's value and freedom. When an individual accepts Jesus as Savior and regeneration takes place, one of the first results is evidence of the fruit of the Spirit (Gal. 5:22–23), among which is to be found "love . . . and gentleness." When these virtues are present, there is a near balance in the scales of the relationship of the sexes, more like the conditions God intended to exist. In like manner, it is only the presence of the Savior, Jesus Christ, that removes the sting of death.

Direct Dealing with God

Until now in this study we have only seen the judgment that has come as the direct effect of the presence of sin in the human race. Treating the effect caused by a problem, any problem, can never provide a final solution. To make a judgment of this nature always leaves the cause of the problem untouched and, therefore, unresolved. The cause of the problem that confronted our first parents was

The First Dispensation

disobedience to the command of God, which when put in its simplest form, is sin, and God hates sin. The crux of this story in the opening chapters of the Bible is the introduction of sin and death into the human sphere. Sin and death are inseparable twins; they are always together. Neither is ever found alone. The Bible says,

> Wherefore, as by one man sin entered into the world, and death by sin, so death passed upon all men, for all have sinned. (Rom. 5:12)

The counterpoint that brings a semblance of balance to the recorded event is that God unilaterally provided an adequate solution to the now exposed, vulnerable, guilty, and condemned parties. Adam and Eve made an attempt to solve their deficiencies by sewing together a covering of fig leaves, and then hoped that God would approve their efforts. God did not leave them long to labor in this misguided endeavor, but very shortly showed them the futility of their thinking. He made acceptable provision for them, which consisted of coverings or clothes made of animal skins. Thus, He furnished an illustration for a spiritual axiom that later would be put into writing and included in the canon of Scripture. This axiom now reads, ". . . without the shedding of blood there is no remission [of sin]" (Heb. 9:22). *Remission* means payment, it means settlement, it means release. This axiom is empirical in nature, and it extends all through the history of man. When first seen, it was in the form of an illustration in Genesis. Next it is found in an Old Testament quotation which says, "The soul that sinneth, it shall die" (Ezek. 18:4). Then it is also found in the New Testament, which proceeds to stress the same theme by saying, "For the wages of sin is death . . ." (Rom. 6:23). There is no alternative; sin *always* results in death. Sin is never forgiven or passed over. Sins, which are *iniquities*, can be forgiven (1 John 1:9). Sin, which is the root cause, can only be paid for by death.

Sin always ends in the death of the perpetrator, unless he has an adequate substitute to die in his place. This is the reason for the coming of Jesus into the world. He came to give His life as a substitute for any man who would accept Him and believe in Him. Because Jesus is God, He is infinite in nature and character. Thus His infinite life and blood is of far greater value than the sum total of the value of all the sinful, finite men of all time. It was because of this fact that Jesus was capable of dying for the sin of the whole world of men and is able to save any and all who come to Him.

The coat of skins that God provided Adam, tells by inference that some animal died, giving up its lifeblood, that the requirement God made might be temporarily satisfied. This could only be a partial solution. It awaited the death of Christ to completely fulfill the righteous demands of a holy God. The blood of an animal could only cover sin for a time; it took the blood of the Savior to remove sin forever (Heb. 10:4).

The last act of this episode occurred when the Lord drove Adam and his wife out of the paradise of Eden into the world outside the garden. He then placed angels in position to prevent their return. This was done to forestall any attempt by fallen man to gain access to the Tree of Life (Gen. 3:24). Open access to the fruit of the Tree of Life would enable men to physically live forever in these present bodies of flesh that are occupied by a sinful nature. That possibility is exactly what God purposed to prevent. It is diffi-

The First Dispensation

cult, if not impossible, for men to foresee the futility and the downright unthinkable results of living endless lives in their present sinful state. If God had allowed Adam to remain in Eden, and thus have had continued access to the Tree of Life, the conditions on earth would have become much more intolerable than they are under the present situation. Men would have lived forever in the deplorable conditions in which the masses of society find themselves today. It isn't the physical part of man that would present the deterrent, but rather the corrupt soul that occupies the body. After all, the body was not changed one whit at the entrance of sin; but man obtained a fallen, sinful nature that is in open rebellion against God.

Man's mortality became an active ingredient as soon as he was denied access to the Tree of Life. The process of aging would now continue to its inevitable end: The body would wear out and no longer be able to sustain the life that dwelled within. The Tree of Life contained some wonderful component, placed there by an edict of God, that allowed the physical part of man to remain youthful, strong, healthy, and vigorous as long as it was obtainable. Not only was the fruit of the tree beneficial, but the leaves, too, had a miraculous effect on men. Ezekiel 47:12 tells of their medicinal quality. Just how long a period an individual could go without partaking of this fruit is now a moot question, for during the time the tree was fully accessible the fruit would quickly become a staple of one's diet.

Man has long sensed the existence of a potion or substance that could sustain physical life. History books used to attest to the truth of this adage by teaching that one of the powers that drove men on in their explorations of the new world (Western Hemisphere) was the hope they would find the Fountain of Youth. This is no longer considered to be politically correct and so has been deleted from all source material being taught in the present generation.

In eternity, men will once again have free and easy admittance to this tree for the Book of Revelation says:

> And he showed me a pure river of water of life, clear as crystal, proceeding out of the throne of God and of the Lamb. In the midst of the street of it, and on either side of the river, was there the Tree of Life, which bore twelve kinds of fruits, and yielded her fruit every month; and the leaves of the tree were for the healing of the nations. (Rev. 22:1–2)

Because of the greatly enlarged population, there will be many trees of life available to accommodate the greater need expressed by the expanded numbers of mankind. The verse quoted would indicate that the Tree of Life grew on both banks of the river.

As the first age came to a close, mankind failed to attain to a state of righteousness, and this prepared the way for God to introduce the second stage of His overall plan.

Chapter 4

The Second Dispensation

The second age has been defined by students as being the Dispensation of Conscience. It was a rather lengthy period of time extending from the fall of Adam until the disaster of the flood of Noah's time. According to Bishop Usher, the age lasted just over 1,650 years. The experience that Adam went through produced something new in man; something he did not have at his creation. This something new was an active conscience. Adam may have been created with a potential conscience but it was dormant until this time. Now he had a fully awakened, mature conscience; and he was no longer innocent, but he knew right from wrong. This fact is illustrated by Adam's embarrassment and his attempt to hide from God among the trees in the garden. He knew he had acted improperly when he knowingly disobeyed his Creator.

Webster's Dictionary defines conscience as follows:

> Moral consciousness in general: the activity or faculty by which distinctions are made between right and wrong

in one's conduct and character; the act or power of moral discrimination; ethical judgment or sensibility, conformity in conduct to one's conceptions of right and wrong.

This assertion of "one's conception of right and wrong" would lead to the conclusion that an infant is born with an inactive, but potential, conscience—one that would require training and shaping from the earliest moments of conscious existence. The parents, and the society to which the child is born would be the two main sources from which the child would draw information, from which the formation of its conscience would proceed. Once formed, the conscience would never vary. This is further proof that the early formative years of a child's life are the most crucial of their existence.

Anthropologists have observed widely diverse judgments of the rightness or wrongness of various types of behavior among nationals of differing countries. That which is considered to be ethically justifiable in one area may be determined offensive and sinful in another. It becomes apparent that children are not born with a fully activated conscience—one that will instantly indicate to them, without fail, what is intrinsically right or wrong.

THE STATE OF MAN AT THE BEGINNING

The state of man at the beginning of this dispensation was one in which he now had an active conscience. It was through this conscience that he received and retained a concept of the knowledge of good and evil. Adam was an adult at the time he received his conscience, and it was probably fully operational from the moment of reception.

The Second Dispensation

Of equal significance, he also was back in fellowship with God, after God had made adequate provision to cover his sin. Worship through a blood offering was installed at this time, as seen in the conduct and experience of the second generation.

Cain and Abel were the sons of Adam, and both were aware of the need to approach God through the medium of sacrifice. In the brothers' experience this ordinance of a blood offering to the Lord was the most serious occasion they would have to encounter. Being vegetarian in their eating habits (Gen. 2:9, 16), the slaying of a creature, with the resulting spilling of blood, was foreign to their nature, and therefore probably abhorrent to them. This fact alone would make it much easier for Cain to bring a bloodless offering of the things he had tenderly nurtured and raised from the ground. Nevertheless this was contrary to the instructions they had received from the Lord. That each of the brothers brought an offering is indicative that they knew it was required of them to do so.

In time they each came before the Lord bearing their sacrificial gift. Cain did not bring a blood offering, and the Bible says in Genesis 4:5, "But for Cain and for his offering He [God] had no regard." This made Cain very angry. In Genesis 4:6–7 God made the situation clear, for the account reads,

> The Lord said to Cain, "Why are you angry? And why has your countenance [face] fallen? If you do well, surely you will be accepted. And if you do not do well, sin is crouching at the door; and its desire is for you, but you must master it.

The emphasis here is that men were to do good and abstain from evil. In short, now that man had an active conscience, he was to live by it. Man's responsibility in this second age can be seen in the Adamic Covenant. Most of these issues have been covered in the judgments that brought the former dispensation to a close.

The Adamic Covenant

The Adamic Covenant applied to the whole human race and is still functional to this day. Nothing has occurred in human history to abrogate that which was initiated at the beginning of the second dispensation. The salient parts of the covenant are:

1. *The serpent was cursed and made to crawl in the dust.* Many varieties of the serpent are poisonous and deadly but all are shunned and even feared by most humans
2. *God gave the promise of a coming Redeemer.* Jesus partially fulfilled the promise at His first advent and will complete the promise at His second advent
3. *The changed state of the woman.* She would suffer pain in childbirth. She would be subservient to her husband and he would rule over her
4. *The earth is cursed for man's sake.* It would bring forth thorns and thistles (and weeds). It would only yield its good with great labor
5. *The sorrow of life.* Without Christ, life can be a heavy burden and hopeless, some find it not worth living. Suicide seems to be a way out

The Second Dispensation

6. *Burdensome labor.* Man can only find a living by toil and sweat
7. *Physical death.* "It is appointed unto man once to die." There is no escape

Living by one's conscience can be a very risky business, as illustrated in this second age. The first person born into this world under this period of testing became a murderer and then a wandering outcast. What happened to his conscience? As a contrast, Enoch, who lived in the seventh generation after Adam, was one of the most godly men of all time. The testimony this man left behind is one every man should strive to emulate, "he walked with God" (Gen. 5:22, 24).

Conscience proved to be an undependable and widely variable guide to a life of righteousness and godliness. There are many good reasons why the individual's conscience could be askew from that of God's standard of righteousness. A man's conscience may be trained wrong in his infancy, due to the culture in which he was born. He may have a weak resolve, whereby his conscience may be bent or twisted and warped out of shape by various degrees of temptation. He may, in a high fit of passion, override or even break a conscience that otherwise has demonstrated itself to be perfectly normal. Cain may be an example of this last type. This second dispensation revealed the devastating weakness and failure of ordering one's life by a conscience that may not be truly or fully dependable.

The disastrous end of this period of testing, which God allowed to continue for more than sixteen centuries, proved to be a calamity for nearly all involved. As the period progressed, man's sin became greater and greater. Sin has a way of multiplying itself, as each successive generation becomes more extreme than the one that preceded it. From the outset of his rebellion against God, Satan has been an active adversary of the Lord and His program, especially of the part that embraces man. In fallen man, Satan has often found an ally who, either willingly or by duplicity, aids his program in defying the Creator.

In the latter half of this dispensation, an unusual phenomenon began to be seen—fallen angels were to be observed mingling among men. The Bible tells the story,

> That the sons of God [angels] saw the daughters of men that they were fair; and they took them wives of all whom they chose. . . . There were giants in the earth in those days; and also after that, when the sons of God came in unto the daughters of men, and they bore children to them, the same became mighty men. . . . And God saw that the wickedness of man was great in the earth, and that every imagination of the thoughts of his heart was only evil continually. (Gen. 6:2, 4–5)

This unnatural liaison between angels and humans produced offspring that were supernatural. Some Bible teachers refuse to believe this passage relates to angels. They say it is only speaking of two different branches of the human race. They say the sons of Seth's branch (godly) married daughters of Cain's branch (ungodly) and the children from this union were superhuman. If this were true then any mixed marriage today between a Christian and an unbeliever would have the same result: a child with superhuman physical abilities. We know this to be untrue. Even the marriage of a demon-possessed person does not create progeny of unnatural physical size or prowess.

The Second Dispensation

Giants! Even the name brings forth visions of great exploits, of accomplishments and victories beyond our own and known capabilities. Every nation and people has stories, folktales, and lore about giants. Are these just figments of a runaway imagination? Are they just simple, interesting stories to fascinate children? Or is there a core of truth deep behind the thought? Giants! The Bible tells of three different periods in the distant past when giants were actual figures who walked among men.

The first instance is the one under observation in this study and recorded in Genesis 6 which took place in Noah's time. We have seen where the Scripture said, "there were giants in the earth in those days; and also after that . . ." The last phrase of that quote from Genesis is preparing the way to tell of there being giants on earth in Moses' and Joshua's time (Num. 13:22, 33), and again in David's time (1 Sam. 17:4). This business of angels mingling with men is serious trouble indeed.

Someone has asked, were all giants evil? This was answered with the use of another question, Are all unbelievers evil? We know that in the eyes of the Lord, according to the third chapter of the Book of Romans, all unbelievers are declared to be unrighteous and, therefore, unholy (Rom. 3:10). Furthermore, John 3:18 says that such an individual stands condemned already. The question of evil in this instance is shown to be moot, for it is both hypothetical and debatable.

When angels mixed with humans, immediately the bloodline of the offspring became contaminated with an element that was foreign and nonhuman. A contaminated bloodstream—we are just discovering the critical danger that lies in that situation in our generation. One key to understanding the seriousness of this eventuality may be found in the passage of Genesis 6:9. There it is written that Noah was "perfect in his generations." The Bible does not say Noah was perfect as an individual, but rather he was "perfect in his generations." The primary use of the word *generations* in Scripture is in reference to genealogical registry, and thus the inference of this passage is that Noah was free of any blood contamination due to his forebears. Apparently this contamination by angelic beings had been occurring over a long enough period of time that Noah was the single person of his generation that was left untouched by it.

There is a close parallel to this story occurring in contemporary society. The human bloodstream has been invaded by a deadly virus known as HIV. This condition often results in a disease called AIDS, for which there is no known cure. It is considered to be a terminal illness. Scientists believe they have traced the blight back to its source, but in a few short years there are many millions of people all around the world who have been infected by this blood contamination. The very latest word from those fighting the disease is that, in some countries, up to 40 percent of the population is infected.

When the human bloodstream was contaminated by an outside source, and that being angelic, God determined there was but one way to correct the problem. He had to make sure the contamination was passed on no further. The only way that could be guaranteed was to eliminate the carrier. The moment we consider this, we have before us the major reason for the worldwide flood of Noah's time.

The same series of events are again seen to unfold in Joshua's time. The Bible says there were giants in the land,

The Second Dispensation

but on this occasion they were confined to the seven nations that occupied the land of Canaan (Deut. 7:1–2). Just as it was with the flood in Noah's experience, God knew there was only one sure way to stop the corrupting plague. The order was given to Joshua and to Israel to wipe out those nations—men, women, and children. The question may be asked, Why destroy the innocent babies and the young children? They are surely harmless. Yet in those small bodies flowed blood that was contaminated with the non-human elements, which, if left alone, would soon corrupt the entire race. This may seem to some to be an awfully strong and harsh antidote, but God knew it was the only way. What God does is just and good and right.

The New Testament Book of Jude adds some weight to the foregoing account when its author writes,

> And the angels who kept not their first estate, but left their own habitation, he hath reserved in everlasting chains under darkness unto the judgment of the great day. Even as Sodom and Gomorrah, and the cities about them in like manner, giving themselves over to fornication, and going after strange flesh, are set forth for an example, suffering the vengeance of eternal fire. (Jude :6–7).

This passage relates to those fallen angels who left their own sphere of habitation to invade another that was foreign to them. They did this under the drive of licentiousness and unnatural desire. The passage quoted above says "in like manner." In Sodom they desired to engage in fornication.

At this point some will say, "But angels are sexless." That statement is not scripturally verified. What the Bible actually says about angels is that they do not marry, nor are they given in marriage (see Mark 12:25). The key purpose of marriage is procreation and to provide a safe, loving, closed environment in which to raise children. The Bible indicates God fully intended the family unit to be the keystone upon which all human society should be built. Destroy the family, and you will surely destroy society. In comparison, there is a fixed number of angels, and they do not die as do humans. They have no need to procreate to continue their existence. This effectively eliminates the need for marriage among them.

Not all fallen angels are of this group that are chained and awaiting judgment. Satan has a multitude of followers, of whom many are still free to roam about and carry out his various schemes. These are the ones that mostly contact men and are commonly called *demons*. The New Testament gives quite a number of instances of Jesus encountering various members of this fractious horde, who are under the command of the devil.

Men are warned by God that "... we wrestle not against flesh and blood, but against principalities, against powers, against the rulers of the darkness of this world, against spiritual wickedness in high places" (Eph. 6:12). The division of the fallen angels as given in this verse of Scripture would seem to indicate the fallen ones are not all of the same class or authority. This would lead to the conclusion that, like the military, the members of the angelic sphere are of different rank—the sequence going from private to general officer, with each having its corresponding dominion.

The angels that are chained would seem to be the ones who left their own habitation and interfered in the affairs and the sphere of humans. There appears to be a significant difference between a demon who takes a human body as a host in a clear-cut situation of demon possession; and that of a demon who takes on the characteristics of a man and who acts, walks, and lives as a man in the realm where men live. There seems to be a special judgment reserved for the fallen angels who exercised insubordination to this degree. During the millennial kingdom, the members of the Church, the Bride of Christ, will sit in judgment on these recalcitrant heavenly beings. God's Word presents the question to the New Testament saint, "Don't you know that we shall judge angels?" (1 Cor. 6:3).

The Close of the Dispensation

After centuries of endeavoring to walk the path of righteousness and producing good works by using the conscience as his guide, man's absolute failure is beyond any reasonable attempt to dispute. Indeed, it proved to be a fiasco of major proportions. It was under conscience in the second dispensation, and again under law in the fifth age, that man approached the line of no return in regard to the continued existence of the human race. At the end of the second age the race of men nearly all perished in the waters of a worldwide flood. At the end of the fifth age, the race is again put in peril—this time by days of tribulation and affliction, a time of wrath such as the world has never encountered before (Mark 13:19–20). God, in His grace, shortened the time of destruction, lest the Jewish people be wiped out and His promises to them be negated. Conscience has proven itself to be too weak and vacillating an element to keep men in the right relationship with God. A conscience must be trained. Too often this training is in the wrong direction and, thus, produces the wrong result.

In Noah's day, morality had degenerated to the point where the collective thought and intent of society as a whole was only toward evil, antigodly, in all its decisions. In Genesis 6:1–7, 11–13 it is said that the wickedness of man was great. This was chiefly observed by the fact the thoughts of men's hearts were only evil continually. As this became more and more of a reality, it grieved the heart of God. Despite history and the result of past actions, man's heart has not changed one whit. Because of the depravity of the heart, the actions of men could only be evil, for the Bible says in Proverbs 4:23, "Keep your heart with all diligence; for out of it are the issues of life." Even more importantly and to the point, the Bible also says,

> A good man, out of the good treasure of his heart, brings forth that which is good; and an evil man, out of the evil treasure of his heart, brings forth that which is evil; for of the abundance of the heart his mouth speaks. (Luke 6:45)

Man's condition is certainly a point to ponder when the Bible says, "The earth was filled with violence" (Genesis 6:11–13).

Satan's purpose in all this activity was to corrupt the race through which God had promised a coming Savior (Gen. 3:15). He mainly stayed in the background and worked through his followers, some of the fallen angels. Satan is not omniscient, but he does know the Scripture, and it is through that medium he is made aware of God's promise of a future Messiah. The entire thrust of Satan's activity was to invalidate God's promise and His Word.

Man's unrighteousness resulted in God's judgment, which took the form of a worldwide flood. All life on the

The Second Dispensation

earth was destroyed, and only in the ark was life spared. God always has a faithful few, a righteous remnant, whom He chooses to protect, keep, and thus validate His promises (Gen. 6:8–9). God sets limits on the judgments He ordains, both as to the subjects who must undergo them and to the length of time each judgment will be in effect. It should disturb and alert all believers to the things taking place now, for Jesus Himself said, "And as it was in the days of Noah, so shall it be also in the days of the Son of man. . . . Even thus shall it be in the day, when the Son of man is revealed" (Luke 17:26, 30).

The time of which the Lord spoke is approaching with incredible speed. Moral standards are changing faster than one can remain informed. The ethical measure of Noah's time could not have been greatly different from that of the present generation. All over the world the value of the family is being downgraded. Taking its place are such questionable values as alternate lifestyles, personal rights, same-sex marriages, homosexuality, along with the use of all types of drugs. These things are becoming more and more socially tolerated, and in many instances they are being legally defended. Satanic worship is becoming more common, and the news is rife with stories of unnatural appearances, strange voices, and things that seemingly move about on their own initiative. On the crime scene, rape and murder are rampant—everyday occurrences. Those guilty of such affronts to organized society have no trouble finding professional men ready to defend them, and often escape justice entirely. Just as it took direct punitive action by the Lord to correct the affairs of men in the world of Noah's day, so will it require the same type of antidote to correct the ills of today. The person of the Lord, in His second appearance on planet Earth, is the only sure, viable solution to the web of problems in which our race has enmeshed itself. When the Lord appears again on earth He will come in the role of "the righteous Judge," and no decision will be too great for Him.

Despite this abject failure of men—in the test for righteousness conducted in this second dispensation—other men have, down through the ages, insisted they must be allowed to live as their conscience directs. There have been conscientious objectors to one thing or another in every generation, including the present one. This has been a source of trouble, hardship and at times tragedy as men persist in their supposed right to make this demand. The only successful walk that will result in "right doing" is to walk in the light of the instructions God has given in His Word, the Bible.

The Judgment

> It is a fearful thing to fall into the hands of the Living God. (Heb. 10:31)

The judgment that befell mankind at the end of the Dispensation of Conscience was the most catastrophic in the history of the race. God brought about a worldwide flood that destroyed all living things on the face of the earth, with the exception of those who found refuge in the vessel that God had instructed Noah to build. Many world scientists since that day denounce the truth of a flood of this magnitude and dispute all evidence that supports such an event.

The Second Dispensation

Men know little of pre-Flood conditions on earth. Apart from the biblical account of the event, a hard, factual record is all but nonexistent. The slant of higher education, along with the bias of the media, causes the Bible to be looked at as less than true and exact. The aim and purpose of this study is to reveal what the Bible does say and let the facts fall where they will. The Bible says in its opening chapter,

> And God said, "Let there be an expanse between the waters to separate water from water." So God made the expanse and separated [bisected] the water under the expanse from the water above it. And it was so. God called the expanse "sky." . . . And God said, "Let the water under the sky be gathered to one place, and let dry ground appear." And it was so. (Gen. 1:6–10, NIV)

Assuming the Bible to be a true and accurate account, then it is to be believed that half the water associated with the earth was hung in a curtain or a canopy above the atmosphere that surrounds the globe. This period of time and the events allocated to it should rightly be called the *six days of restoration* and not the *six days of creation,* as is commonly done.

It was at this time that dry land appeared and the scene was set for the existence of warm-blooded creatures. Scientists teach that water is a very good insulator. With this fact in mind, a canopy of water around the earth would be the principle cause of a constant semitropical temperature worldwide. The heat from the sun's rays, as it struck the surface of the earth, would be trapped under the canopy of water, and the whole atmosphere would be heated uniformly. Scientists today boast that they have found the residue of tropical or semitropical plants and trees in all parts of the earth, including Antarctica.

There would be a lack of hot or cold areas, and thus there would be no wind and no storms. It is a fact that hot air rises, creating a void. The movement of cold air rushing in to displace it is what we know as wind. The greater the differential of temperature between the hot and cold air, the fiercer the storm. The record in Genesis specifically states that there was no rain, but a mist went up from the earth to water the ground (Gen. 2:5–6).

There is a second vital factor involved in this complex system that God put into operation. Water is also an excellent filter. This canopy, when in place, would filter out the dangerous and harmful ultraviolet rays from sunlight with the net result that men would live healthier, longer lives. The canopy of water would be the natural sunblock of its day. The fact of long life spans as being normal for that dispensation is verified in the generational records of Genesis 5. There it is recorded that it was not uncommon for men to live hundreds of years.

Of the half of the water that was left under the atmosphere, on the surface of the earth, God said, "Let the waters below the heavens be gathered in one place . . . and it was so" (Gen. 1:9). If this is a true translation of the original statement, then it is highly possible there was only one ocean in the pre-Flood era. This ocean would have been like a very large lake surrounded on all sides by dry ground.

The second dispensation ended with tremendous destruction, and the havoc extended both to the race and to its environment. The living God is known for His longsuffering and mercy, but He is also a God of justice and wrath. When the activity of Satan, coupled with the sinful-

The Second Dispensation

ness of man, reached the point of jeopardizing the truth of God and put His promises at risk, it was time for intervention. The Lord first gave Noah careful instruction as to the procedures he was to take in order to escape the soon-coming judgment that would destroy all living things on the earth. After Noah was obedient to all of God's instructions, God was free to act. The sovereign, omnipotent one then reached out and touched the earth both high and low. The Bible says in very simple terms,

> ... the same day were all the fountains of the great deep broken up, and the windows of heaven were opened. And the rain was upon the earth forty days and forty nights. (Gen. 7:11–12)

Between these two extremes—the breaking up of the deep parts of the ocean along with the dismantling of the canopy of water overhead—enough water was provided to cover the earth with a layer fifteen cubits deep (22.5 ft.) at the highest mountain tops. The surface of the earth is made up of a series of land masses called tectonic plates. These plates are like floating islands on the sea of molten magma that constitutes the core of the planet. As these tectonic plates jostle and rub against each other in their movements, the surface undergoes vibrations that men have come to know as earthquakes. The harder the bump, the more severe the quake. When the deepest parts of the ocean were broken up (filled in), the logical counteraction would be the dropping of the mountains to much lower elevations. Following forty days and forty nights of this type of catastrophic movement—unprecedented seismic action—the surface of the earth would be much smoother, like a ball. Under these circumstances the amount of water available would easily cover the earth's surface to the depth mentioned.

It is difficult for the human mind to conceive the erosion that occurred when the water first washed over the land mass. Then, little more than a year later, it proceeded to flow off again as the land heaved up to its present configuration. The hydraulic action of moving water is fierce and frightening to observe, especially when close at hand. Millions, even billions, of gallons of water pouring off the continents could easily account for the great canyons that are found on every continent. With the many megatons of water in movement there would be megatons of mud, silt, detritus, and other materials washed along with it. Vast tracts of forest would be knocked down and, in many instances, buried deeply beneath flood debris. Great herds of animals, of all types, would suffer a like fate. Pictures of the African Serengeti Plain of today show huge herds of animals as far as the eye can see. The history of the United States says that fifteen million bison once roamed North America as late as the eighteen hundreds. It is quite possible there were comparable herds of various types of animals in many parts of earth at the time of the great Flood. The coal and oil fields that are found so valuable to society today may well have been laid down in a time of God's judgment upon a former society that existed in Noah's day. Most of the separation of water and land would occur in the first months following the flood, but it is entirely possible that it took a period of years. In fact, at a far-reduced rate, it could be a continuing process going on yet today.

The judgment of this time did not cease with the punishment of the race, but God also dealt with the fallen angels that wandered away from their own prescribed area of activity. The apostle Peter writes,

The Second Dispensation

> For if God spared not the angels that sinned, but cast them down to hell, and delivered them into chains of darkness, to be reserved unto judgment; and spared not the old world, but saved Noah, the eighth person, a preacher of righteousness, bringing in the flood upon the world of the ungodly . . . (2 Pet. 2:4–5)

God hates sin. In many quarters the statement "God hates" is totally and completely found to be unacceptable. It has often been said that the God of the Old Testament was a harsh and cruel God, full of hatred and just waiting for men to step out of line so He could expend His fury on them. In comparison, these same teachers are prone to say the New Testament tells of a God Who practices love and forgiveness and whose focal point is one of compassion. Such a person fails to see that the Bible is speaking of the same God, but one Who is working in an entirely different dispensation and with an entirely different set of principles. God does not exercise any one of His attributes at the expense of another. God's wrath and His hatred are still parallel and coexisting attributes of His person and are fully expressed in the New Testament. It is a strange fact that the same chapter that contains what many believe to be the best known and loved verse in the Bible, John 3:16, also ends with a dire warning of wrath, John 3:36:

> He that believes on the Son has everlasting life; and he that believes not the Son shall not see life, but the wrath of God abides on him.

The New Testament is replete with references to God's wrath, which is said to be held in restraint only while He is making the riches of His glory known to the believers of this age, who make up the Church.

> What if God, willing to show his wrath and make his power known, endured with much longsuffering the vessels of wrath fitted to destruction; and that he might make known the riches of his glory on the vessels of mercy, which he had before prepared unto glory, even us, whom he has called . . . (Rom. 9:22–24)

The Bible says, and experience shows, that God is longsuffering; but one day His patience will end. Then His wrath will be exposed for all unbelievers and Christ rejecters to see.

> And [they] said to the mountains and rocks, Fall on us, and hide us from the face of him that sits on the throne, and from the face of the Lamb; for the great day of his wrath is come, and who shall be able to stand? (Rev. 6:16–17)

> And I heard a great voice out of the temple saying to the seven angels, Go your ways, and pour out the bowls of wrath of God upon the earth. (Rev. 16:1)

> And out of his mouth goes a sharp sword, that with it he should smite the nations, and he shall rule them with a rod of iron; and he treads the winepress of the fierceness and wrath of Almighty God. (Rev. 19:15)

Where sin arises, judgment will soon follow. No creature, regardless of status, has ever, or will ever, escape paying the penalty the wrath of a holy God demands.

Chapter 5

The Third Dispensation

The third dispensation began with a world situation diverse from all others. It was a new beginning in almost every aspect of human existence. Enormous changes would have taken place in the earth's surface. The only way the various continents could emerge from under the blanket of water that covered them was through the action of gigantic earthquakes, as the tectonic plates that comprise the earth's crust moved in their relationship one to another. Some plates would rise and break the surface of the water to become continents. Other plates dropped to form the depths of the oceans. This movement of the earth's crust would undoubtedly create great heat, and some volcanic action would be the result. In this manner, great and rugged mountain ranges would be thrust up. Thus, amid much chaos and at the expenditure of tremendous amounts of energy, the continents and oceans were formed. For the first time the earth and its topography would be much as we see and know it today.

With the loss of the water canopy that had formerly surrounded the earth, there was now twice as much water on the surface to form the seas and oceans, just as modern charts and maps show them. Sunlight was now able to come directly to the earth's surface without being filtered through the canopy. The earth experienced definite seasons for the first time, with their accompanying variations of heat and cold, which in turn brought wind and storm.

This is the time the poles received their ice caps, as they became the more difficult parts of the earth's surface for the sun's rays to reach. Vast amounts of water are in storage in the ice caps at the north and south extremities of the earth. Scientists have said that if this ice melted the mean high-water mark of the world's oceans would raise a little over twenty feet. This is just one of the ways God used in bringing the dry land, the continents, into being. Another result of the loss of the water-canopy filter is that the destructive parts of the sun's rays, the ultraviolet, now had free access to the earth's surface; man's life span was dramatically shortened. With the new environment, the population was begun anew with just eight individuals present– Noah and his wife with their three sons and their wives.

Noah's first action upon debarking on firm dry ground, after being afloat for more than a year, was to build an altar and offer a sacrifice to the Lord for safety and deliverance. Noah was a very godly man, and he was in fellowship and communication with the Lord all his life. He is one of only two men in the Old Testament of whom it is recorded that they "walked with God" (Gen. 6:9). He also had the encomium of being all that God commanded him: "Thus did Noah; according to all that God commanded him, so did he" (Gen. 6:22). This is the age that has been called the

Dispensation of Human Government, because God said in effect, "here is a new, cleansed and purified earth, a new start; see what you can do with it." Human responsibility before God for this era is seen in detail in the Noahic Covenant.

The Noahic Covenant

This covenant is the third of a series and is called *the everlasting covenant*. It is not only made with man, but also with every living creature on the earth (Gen. 9:16–17). To make doubly sure there would be no mistake as to its importance, God said this covenant would be for "perpetual generations" with every living thing (Gen. 9:12). The point to be stressed is this covenant is very much in force to this day. Men break this covenant at their own peril. There are seven primary points to the covenant, and they are:

1. *Be fruitful, multiply and fill the earth.* This is a reiteration of the first point of the first covenant. There is a growing concern over this issue today as it relates to the overpopulation of the earth. Strong attempts are being made to overthrow this command
2. *The fear of man is upon all living things.* Man originally was to have dominion; now it is changed to fear
3. *All flesh is given to man to eat.* Man was originally created a vegetarian, but now he becomes a meat-eater, and thus he also becomes a hunter
4. *Man is not to eat blood.* While meat is permitted to eat, blood becomes a forbidden item

5. *Man is not to slay man, under threat of capital punishment.* Until this time, murder was an iniquity, but now it is a transgression and thus punishable by death. Man has chosen to ignore this point of covenanted conduct to the detriment of society
6. *All flesh shall never again be destroyed by flood.* There have been many local and extremely damaging floods in various areas of the world, but nothing on a global scale
7. *The earth shall never again be destroyed by flood*

These seven points constitute the everlasting covenant. As long as the earth exists, this covenant will be in force. God gave the rainbow as a token of the covenant, and the Bible says whenever *He* sees the rainbow *He* will remember the covenant and abide by it.

The Length and Course of the Dispensation
The length of time consumed by the third dispensation, according to Bishop Usher's chronology, was 427 years. It extended from the time of the Flood until the confusion of languages that took place at Babel. During the course of this age a number of very unique things had their beginning, and man has had to struggle with them ever since.

Noah, in his pre-Flood existence was a vegetarian, like all his neighbors, and most likely much of his life was spent as a gardener or a farmer. This would undoubtedly mean he was familiar with a vineyard and the grapes grown there, along with their byproduct, grape juice. Following the Flood he would naturally have reproduced his vineyard to again enjoy its fruit and its juice. But something unexpected happened. For the first time, his grape juice was subject to direct sunlight, and fermentation took place. A brief search in the *Encyclopedia Americana* finds the definition of fermentation stated as, "the name given to the general class of chemical changes or decompositions produced in organic substrates through the activity of enzymes elaborated by living microorganisms." Furthermore, it says: "Phosphorylation is necessary in every type of fermentation." This chemical action begins with the absorption of some form of energy, other than heat energy, generated from an external source. The ultraviolet rays from the sun, no longer filtered out by the water canopy, prove to be that outside source of energy serving to excite or activate the enzymes in grape juice, causing fermentation to begin.

Noah must have detected a different taste to his beverage, but as it was new and far from objectionable, he continued to drink. As the story goes, he became very drunk. The irony of this story is that one of the most godly men spoken of in the Old Testament became the first man recorded to be drunk. Drinking and drunkenness have been a major problem for men since that time. There is no account that God ever censured or punished Noah for this episode.

There is another side to this unsavory event, which led to far more serious consequences, and it has to do with Noah's younger son, Ham. In his inebriated state, Noah lost both his inhibitions and his modesty; but Ham lost his discretion and his parental reverence. Jewish tradition says that Noah's grandson Canaan was the first of the family to see Noah in this condition of immodesty. Then in conjunction with his father, Ham, they caused a scene that was inappropriate to the occasion. In the aftermath of this humiliating experience, and reacting to the demeaning conduct of his youngest son along with that of his grandson, Noah said, "Cursed be Canaan; a servant of servants shall he be unto his brethren" (Gen. 9:25). It is amazing how some small, unintended, thoughtless incidents can influence the lives of others for centuries to come. This seemingly minor event had major repercussions as far as the alignment of the peoples and the nations of the world would develop. All the future nations of the world would spring from the progeny of Noah's three sons. Because of this single event Noah prophesied that the descendants of one son and grandson would be servants to the descendants of the other two brothers (see Gen. 9:25–27).

There seems to be little doubt among anthropologists that Ham and Caanan are the forebears of the Black race. Some scholars teach that the name *Ham* carries the meaning of "swarthy" or "darkened" and the name *Cush*, Ham's son, means "the black one." This may or may not be true. There are those who go beyond the bounds of Scripture and teach that, because of the curse placed upon Canaan, his descendents would be inferior to the descendents of Shem and Japheth. This goes beyond the rules of good exegesis and should not be expounded.

A second phenomenon that had its beginning in the third dispensation is that of idolatry. In the more than sixteen centuries that had elapsed prior to the Flood, there was ungodliness, atheism, and irreligion practiced among men; but not a single recorded case of idolatry. If men thought in terms of gods at all, it was always of the true God and never of a false god or an imitation god, as is an idol. In the new, purified earth that was turned over to men, along with the power to govern, it did not take a long time for a man like Nimrod to emerge. The Bible says of Nimrod that "he began to be a mighty one in the earth" (Gen. 10:8). He not only set himself up as a king, but he formed the first known empire. The Scripture relates that he ruled over a group of four different cities (Gen. 10:10). His capitol city appears to have been Babel, which later became known as Babylon. In order to better solidify his position as leader and king, he instigated a system of worship in which his subjects would be required to participate. In this manner, idolatry became an organized source of power. Many secular leaders, as well as military men since Nimrod's day, have sought to use similar schemes to either gain power or to consolidate their position of authority. This program worked so well that Satan will use it again with similar success in the Tribulation period to assist the Antichrist in gaining power over the whole world.

Satan's Activity

The system of false religion and idolatry that had its beginning at Babel, has through the intervening centuries been refined and honed, until it has become Satan's primary tool in his attempt to supplant God. It was at Babel where men first built a magnificent tower, formed their own system of worship, and thought they would make their own way to heaven. They thought that God could not refuse the zeal they exhibited, all the pomp and ceremony they could devise, conducted in the most beautiful of surroundings. Surely God was to be pleased by their efforts; it was the best they could do. The Bible says, "There is a way which seemeth right unto a man, but the end thereof are the ways of death" (Prov. 14:12). The system of false worship is often filled with vain and ostentatious displays designed to impress men. This system in its many varied forms is called

Babylonianism, and when placed in comparison with the true Church, is found to be impure, corrupt, unclean, and depraved. The Church is named the spotless Bride of Christ; the false system is referred to as the Harlot and is spiritually filthy.

Babylonianism will continue to flourish until the last days, when a powerful world leader who has the unstinted aid of his equally powerful religious cohort will gain governmental control of all the earth (Rev. 13:7). The true Church will have been caught up to heaven to be a participant in a royal wedding taking place there. All false religion, including the false church, will be left behind on earth. It is the amalgamation of these various groups that will be known as Mystery Babylon (Rev. 17:5–6). What began at Babel in the third dispensation will attain full-flowered maturity following the end of the sixth dispensation. It is at that time Babylonianism will be at its zenith. The enjoyment of this heady experience will be but for a brief moment only, for in the judgments of the Great Tribulation this long lasting but anti-Christal system will be completely destroyed (Rev. 18:8).

The Close of the Dispensation

This dispensation, like the ones before it, ends with the failure of the human element. Man's effort through the ages has been to make himself independent of God. Working toward this end his labor is to establish some permanency to life on earth. He would like nothing more than to establish and prove his self-sufficiency. Man simply cannot abide the thought that he is only a transient being in this life. The words that express his thinking, as seen in Genesis 11, give rise to some provocative reflection. The scripture says,

> And they said, "Come, let us build us a city and a tower, whose top may reach unto heaven; and let us make us a name, lest we be scattered abroad upon the face of the whole earth." (Gen. 11:4)

This verse points our meditations in two diverse directions. First, it reveals that men expended a good portion of their efforts in building a city, an attempt at a permanent base down here. Civilization has always been man's struggle to make a lasting, comfortable dwelling place for himself on this sin-cursed earth. In contrast, the Bible says that the Christian's "citizenship is in heaven." Jesus said, "I go to prepare a place for you" (John 14:2).

Ironically, men have found death to be universal, so they have set about to create their own paradise and a way to get there by their own system of achievements. They have established an imitative system, sometimes a very elaborate system, of worship and sacrifice to a pantheon of man-made deities. It was in this manner idolatry became a definite factor in men's affairs. Natural men spend much time and effort in gaining heaven, or "paradise" by way of their own works. Idolatry has become an additional curse on the human race ever since it was first introduced at Babel.

The second line of thought is initiated by the phrase "let us make us a name." One of the driving forces of human nature is to be recognized as being someone of importance and never to be forgotten by our fellow men. Every cemetery in the land bears witness to this truth in its display of elaborate headstones and special memorials. Men have an insatiable desire that their names live on and they not be forgotten. Vast amounts of wealth, labor, and material have been expended in the attempt to satisfy this drive. There is scarcely a people or a nation since the time of the tower of Babel that has not seen this phenomena in some form. Egypt has its pyramids, India its Taj Mahal, even the United States has its eternal flame in Arlington National Cemetery. There are countless other examples, but in a few short years all suffer the same fate. The departed ones are seldom remembered after their generation has passed away, and they themselves then join the ranks of the unknown.

At Babel, man established a precedent by concentrating his efforts on gaining heaven, or paradise, by way of his own works. God puts an end to this foolishness by coming down personally to view the scene (Gen. 11:5). He appraises the situation and then passes judgment on men by confusing the languages of all those involved (Gen. 11:7). There are thousands of different languages in the world today, all as a direct result of this episode. Giving man free reign to establish his own government and bring in a time of righteousness proved to be another opportunity for man to reveal his wrong thinking in the test to do that which was right, even in the face of the God-given incentive.

Chapter 6

The Fourth Dispensation

With neighbor no longer able to communicate with neighbor, because of the judgment God brought upon the race, strong compulsion was felt by various family groups to migrate to more distant lands. In this manner different language clusters were formed, which in turn led to different nations. All people who spoke the same language and were able to communicate with one another had the tendency to remain close together. As the groups grew in size and numbers they claimed their own autonomous territory, and so different nations began to emerge.

It was in this tumultuous time that God in His sovereignty arbitrarily chose one man, and his subsequent family, to be the witness to all the world of God's person, His love, and His grace, and to be the avenue through which the Savior and salvation should come. God chose the man Abram, even though his family background was one which was engrossed in idolatry. The Bible, in the Old Testament, says,

> Thus says the LORD God of Israel, Your fathers dwelt on the other side of the river [Euphrates] in old time, even Terah, the father of Abraham, and the father of Nahor; and they served other gods. (Josh. 24:2)

Despite this most unfavorable beginning, God knew Abram's heart was fertile ground for the implantation of truth. When God first spoke to Abram He chose to speak to a man who was already a mature and married man.

THE STATE OF MAN AT THE BEGINNING

This dispensation opens with Abraham being at the center of God's attention. Again and again the Bible says the Lord spoke to him and a regular dialogue would ensue (Gen. 12:1; 13:14). There were times when the Lord appeared to him in a vision, as stated in Genesis 15:1. Of greater wonder are those occasions when the Bible says the Lord actually appeared where Abraham could visually see Him. Incredible! Several of these memorable junctures are seen in Genesis (17:1; 18:1, 22) of which one will be quoted as an example:

> And when Abram was ninety-nine years old, the LORD appeared to him, and said unto him, I am the Almighty God; walk before me, and be perfect [sincere]. I will make my covenant between you and me, and will multiply you exceedingly. And Abram bowed low before the LORD; and God talked with him, . . . (Gen. 17:1–3)

These were the days and times when Abraham acquired the sobriquet the "Friend of God" (James 2:23). When Abraham enjoyed this sweet, intimate fellowship with the

The Fourth Dispensation

Lord there were always two objects present to typify his pilgrim character. These objects were a tent and an altar. They are mentioned frequently throughout the story of Abraham, some of the references being Genesis 12:2,8; 13:3-4,18; 26:24-25. The tent represented his temporary status on earth, showing the earth was but a stopover; he was a stranger and a foreigner here. The altar represented Abraham's method of approach and his acceptability to the Lord. He recognized the need and was willing to bring a blood sacrifice to open the way for fellowship and communion with the Divine. This is the standing of every Christian who is living by faith in God's Word, the Bible. When speaking of believers of the past, it says,

> These all died in faith, not having received the promises but having seen them afar off, and were persuaded of them, and embraced them, and confessed that they were strangers and pilgrims on the earth. For they that say such things declare plainly that they seek a country. And truly, if they had been mindful of that country from which they came out, they might have had opportunity to return. But now they desire a better country, that is, an heavenly; wherefore, God is not ashamed to be called their God; for He hath prepared for them a city.
> (Heb. 11:13-17).

The Book of Hebrews says, "For he [Abraham] looked for a city . . . whose builder and maker was God" (Heb. 11:10). What a contrast this is to the men of Babel of the past dispensation, whose desire was to build their own city. They wanted stability and permanency here on earth and without God. Their wish at that time was the same as natural man's anytime—to have control over his own fate.

The Abrahamic Covenant

After God first spoke with him, Abram responded immediately, although it was only in partial obedience to that which God commanded. The original command is given in Genesis 12:1–3 and is in three parts:

1. Get out of your country
2. Get away from your kindred
3. Get away from your father's house (family)

It was not until many years later, at his separation from his nephew Lot (Gen. 13:14), that his obedience was complete. At that time God said, "Now, I will." Yet it was from the moment God first spoke unto Abram that he was in covenant relationship with God. The covenant that is revealed in the conversation God spoke with this man is found in Genesis 12:1–4 and 13:14–17.

The Main Points of the Covenant

1. I will make of you a great nation
2. I will bless you
3. I will make your name great
4. You shall be a blessing
5. I will bless them that bless you
6. I will curse him that curses you
7. In you shall all families of the earth be blessed

This covenant and all that it implies is the main reason for the fourth age to be given the title of the Dispensation of Promise. The covenant itself is called the Abrahamic

The Fourth Dispensation

Covenant and contains a number of times when God said, "*I will.*" He did not institute any conditions to modify the promises contained within the perimeters of these *I will*; thus the covenant as stated stands in the ranks of the unconditional. Furthermore, the Scripture asserts that this covenant, like the one before, is everlasting in its scope (Gen. 17:7–8).

As Abraham grew more mature in his knowledge of God through fellowship with Him, God added other points to the covenant that existed between them. He progressively enlarged upon the blessings He had in store for Abraham. At this stage, He included a land as an inheritance:

> And the LORD said unto Abram, . . . "Lift up now your eyes, and look from the place where you are northward, and southward, and eastward, and westward, for all the land which you see, to you will I give it, and to thy seed forever. And I will make your seed as the dust of the earth, so that if a man can number the dust of the earth, then shall your seed also be numbered. (Gen. 13:14–16)

God later extended the covenant even further, to more specifically cover Abraham's descendents, when He said:

> Neither shall your name any more be called Abram, but your name shall be Abraham; for a father of many nations have I made you. And I will make you exceedingly fruitful, and I will make nations of you, and kings shall come out of you. And I will establish my covenant between me and you and your seed after you in their generations for an everlasting covenant, to be a God unto you and to your seed after you. And I will give unto

you, and to your seed after you, the land wherein you are a sojourner, all the land of Canaan, for an everlasting possession; and I will be their God. (Gen. 17:5–8)

The scope of the Abrahamic Covenant was narrowed to a very significant yet special portion of Abraham's descendents when God said unto Abraham, "in Isaac shall thy seed be called" (Gen. 21:12). Midian, one of Abraham's eight sons (Gen. 25:2), became a bitter enemy of Israel and fought against Gideon during the time of the judges (Judges 7). Ishmael was Abraham's firstborn son and, as such, he occupied a special place. God said of him:

And as for Ishmael, I have heard you: behold, I have blessed him, and will make him fruitful, and will multiply him exceedingly; twelve princes shall he beget, and I will make him a great nation. But my covenant will I establish with Isaac. (Gen. 17:20–21)

The apostle Paul recognized the importance of the statements made by God in this part of the Scripture, and he wrote, "Neither, because they are the seed of Abraham, are they all children, but, in Isaac shall thy seed be called" (Rom. 9:7). Though Isaac was not Abraham's firstborn, he was the child of faith that Abraham had longed for and looked for, as he had been promised by the Lord. The passage goes on to say that Isaac retained the coveted and covenanted position of being the seed of the promise. "But My covenant will I establish with Isaac, whom Sarah shall bear unto thee at this set time in the next year" (Gen. 17:21).

It has been stated that this is an unconditional covenant; time after time God has used the phrase "I will" with no conditions attached. Thus, it can be determined, if God be true and language is a reliable means of communication, that this covenant covers the descendents of Abraham through the child of promise, Isaac, for all time and eternity.

Length and Course of the Dispensation

Even though this fourth age continued for more than four centuries, it ranks as the shortest of the entire series, apart from that of the first. The cardinal responsibility of Abraham and his descendants was to dwell in the land that God promised to show him and give to them (Gen. 12:1b; 13:14–15). To put it concisely, Abraham and his offspring were to dwell in the land, and *there* God would bless them. The land and the blessing went together as a single, undivided unit. To give added depth and strength to this position, God addressed Isaac, Abraham's son, and told him:

> Go not down into Egypt; dwell in the land that I shall tell you of. Sojourn [live] in this land, and I will be with you, and will bless you; for unto you and unto your seed I will give all these countries, and I will perform the oath which I swore unto Abraham your father. (Gen. 26:2–3)

It should be noted that God confirmed this covenant with an oath. Without doubt God intended this family to dwell in the place (land) of blessing.

Man's Failure and Judgment

Jacob was Abraham's grandson, the third generation, and it was in the final years of his life, in a period of great distress, that he gave his approval for the whole family—by this time seventy-two strong—to journey down to Egypt and dwell there. From a man's view, given the circumstances, this may have seemed the right decision; but from God's view it showed an abysmal lack of faith in His promises, a distrust in the Lord's ability to provide for their needs and keep them safe. God, through His foreknowledge, knew that Jacob, while under duress, would cave in to circumstances and move down into Egypt. To save the situation from total disaster, He made a way for Joseph to go ahead of the family into Egypt and prepare the way for their safe arrival.

The move away from the place of blessing proved to be a disaster for the family. Among the Egyptians they were reduced to the lowest of status, and finally to that of outright slavery. This slavery lasted for a period of some four hundred years and grew to become very harsh and bitter. The only good part of this experience is that, in this sheltered environment, they grew from a family into a nation. The Hebrews, for that is the name by which they were known from this time forward, became a nation of slaves to their former Egyptian hosts, who now became their masters.

Judgment was not reserved for the family of Abraham alone. Egypt, too, felt the hand of God's wrath. In the covenant God had made with Abraham, the sixth point was, "I will curse him that curses you." The people of Egypt were the first to feel the full effect of that part of God's promise. After several centuries of living in close proximity to each other, it would be doubtful if at least some of the Egyptian leaders would not have heard of the covenant God had made with the Hebrew people. Toward the end of this age, Moses evoked the name of the Lord (Jehovah) on numerous occasions while disputing with Pharaoh, but Pharaoh treated Jehovah with contempt. It was as if Pharaoh was saying, "The gods of Egypt must be stronger than your God, for you are our slaves." Many people since that time have felt the sting of God's wrath as a result of treating the Hebrews (Jews) unjustly.

Addendum

In the test for righteousness, Abraham certainly moved in the right direction. The Bible says, "Abraham believed God and it was accounted to him for righteousness" (Gen. 15:6). Now Abraham lived several centuries before the law was given to Moses at Mount Sinai, so it would be an impossibility for him to have received this imputed righteousness through the principle of law. The only alternative would be to receive it by faith, a simple belief in God's word alone. This indicates that imputed righteousness is acquired by nothing man can do, but only on what God has done. Thus Abraham becomes an illustration of a Christian under grace rather than that of a Jew under law. The New Testament says,

> Now it was not written for his sake alone, that it was imputed to him, but for us also, to whom it shall be imputed, if we believe on Him that raised up Jesus, our Lord, from the dead. (Rom. 4:23–24)

It should be understood that imputed righteousness is the standing of every believer who is "in Christ" and is received on the same basis that Abraham experienced. Proof of this is seen when God said through the apostle Paul, "Know you, therefore, that they who are of faith, the same are the sons of Abraham. So, then, they who are of faith are blessed with faithful Abraham" (Gal. 3:7, 9).

Chapter 7

The Fifth Dispensation

The Age of Man under Law began with the giving of the Mosaic law at Mt. Sinai and continues until the establishment of the Messianic kingdom, an event that is still future at this writing. The total elapsed time from the beginning to the end of this dispensation is some 3,500 years. The difficulty encountered in establishing a time period for this age is that the sixth dispensation, which is the present ongoing age, occurs entirely within the outer limits of the fifth age. The sixth age interrupts the fifth age, halting it prematurely. However, when the sixth age runs its course and is finished, the fifth age will again be in force and will continue its interrupted flow to its prophesied end. The sixth dispensation is already 2,000 years old; that would leave about 1,500 years as the period of time for the Age of Law. The scriptural references would read Exodus 19:1; Acts 2:1; Revelation 3:22 and 19:11.

Men were in fellowship with God as this dispensation began, just as with all seven of the ages. After having spent more than 400 years in Egypt, the last part of the time in abject slavery, the descendents of Abraham grew from a family of seventy-two into a nation of several million souls. The Hebrews developed in a very protected and closed environment. While in Egypt as slaves they were kept strictly separate from their Egyptian masters. At the same time, Egypt being the most powerful nation of its day, the Hebrews were also kept from incursions by other peoples. Nevertheless, the Lord heard the long bitter wail of this suffering people as they stood under all the indignities heaped upon them by the relentless Egyptians. The Lord's ear is always tuned toward His people, and when they cry for Him and His help, He responds.

It was God's purpose to get this family, now a nation, back into the land He had promised them, back into the place of blessing. His first move was to produce a leader, who turned out to be Moses. When the Hebrew people left Egypt they were a redeemed nation—redeemed by both blood and by power. At the initiation of the Passover, each Hebrew dwelling had the sacrificial blood applied to the two side posts and the upper post of the door; so when the death angel passed over that night he did not stop but passed on by (Exod. 12:7). An important point to understand is that *only* the firstborn of the family was protected by the blood around the door on that fateful night. It was a tragic day for the Egyptians, for there was no protecting blood on the doors of their homes. The Lord said,

> For I will pass through the land of Egypt this night, and will smite all the first-born in the land of Egypt, both man and beast; and against all the gods of Egypt I will execute judgment: I am the LORD. And the blood shall be to you for a token upon the houses where you are; and when I see the blood, I will pass over you, and the

The Fifth Dispensation

plague shall not be upon you to destroy you, when I smite the land of Egypt. (Exod. 12:12–13)

In the process of leaving Egypt, the Hebrews found their true leader was the Lord. His presence was exposed for all to see in a most spectacular way.

> And the LORD went before them by day in a pillar of a cloud, to lead them the way; and by night in a pillar of fire, to give them light; to go by day and night; He took not away the pillar of the cloud by day, nor the pillar of fire by night, from the people. (Exod. 13:21–22)

Having left the more populated portion of Egypt, they camped for the night on the edge of the wilderness. There they found themselves caught between the Red Sea to their front, and the rapidly approaching, very angry, and vengeful Egyptian army to their rear. The Hebrews had been a nation bound in slavery; they were without military training, without arms, and without means of defense. In this position they were fearful for their lives, thinking any survivors would be returned to Egypt once again as slaves. It was at this critical juncture their leader stepped up and spoke:

> And Moses said unto the people, "Fear not, stand still, and see the salvation of the LORD which He will show you today; for the Egyptians whom you have seen today, you will see them again no more forever. The LORD shall fight for you, and you shall hold your peace." (Exod. 14:13–14)

It is an old and well-known story given in Exodus 14 how the LORD divided the Red Sea and made a path to safety for Israel to escape the oncoming Egyptian army. When that army foolishly tried to follow Israel through the sea, God allowed the sea to return to its normal condition; and the entire Egyptian army, to the last man, perished.

Having been set free from the heavy hand, as well as the threat of Egypt, the Hebrews were led by God out into the wilderness, where they came into the vicinity of Mt. Sinai. On the journey this large body of people were not only led by the LORD, but He supplied all the provender they needed to satisfy their hunger and thirst. At this time they were an elect nation, a redeemed people, in covenant relationship with God and in constant fellowship with Him. The relationship between the Lord and this people may be observed to be different from all others—very special and precious. God spoke to the people of Israel from His heart when He said, "You have seen what I did unto the Egyptians, and how I bore you on eagles' wings and brought you unto myself."

Finally arriving at Sinai after an interesting series of events on the way, God called Moses up on the mountain, where a conference between the two was to take place. It was at this time God approached Moses alone with the subject of the Law, and Moses was then to bring it before the people. It is important to recognize the Law was not imposed until it had been divinely proposed and voluntarily accepted by Israel. One of the first words God used and instructed Moses to take to the people was the word *if*. He said, "Now therefore, *if* you will obey my voice indeed, and keep my covenant, then you shall be a special treasure unto me above all people; . . . an holy nation" (Exod. 19:5, italics added). The *if* makes the passage transitional, and this covenant becomes conditional—depending on what the Hebrew people will do. Their intent and desire was great; there was no hesitation on Israel's part in answering the Lord. "And all the people answered together, and said, 'All that the LORD has spoken we will do.' And Moses returned the words of the people unto the LORD" (Exod.19:8). The people took no time for thought or meditation, "no time for consideration—perhaps as people would say in this our age, no time to pray over the situation." The proposal sounded good, so they quickly accepted it, expecting to fill the qualifications by the force of their own will. If only their ability could match their zeal.

THE MOSAIC COVENANT

The covenant containing *the law* is called the Mosaic Covenant and is the first of three covenants God instituted with the nation Israel during the period of the fifth dispensation. The Mosaic Covenant is the only conditional covenant God made with the nation Israel. The second and third of these covenants, when coupled with the Abrahamic Covenant, form a trilogy that acts as a single, all-encompassing, unconditional compact that sets the status under which Israel will occupy the Promised Land. Each of these covenants can stand alone on its own merits; taken together they present an unbreakable compact, dependent on the faithfulness of God only, and are not influenced by the actions of men.

The covenant of the law was never addressed to the Gentiles but is for Israel and their proselytes exclusively. At a much later date, while the Lord was describing the condition of the Gentiles, He said,

> Wherefore, remember that you, being in time past Gentiles in the flesh, . . . that at that time you were without Christ, being aliens from the commonwealth of Israel, and *strangers from the covenants of promise*, having no hope, and without God in the world. (Eph. 2:11–12, italics added)

> For when the Gentiles, who have not the law, do by nature the things contained in the law, these, having not the law, are a law unto themselves. (Rom. 2:14)

The law did not serve to institute right relations between an Israelite and God. Too much importance cannot be placed on the fact that an Israelite was physically born into an elect race, a redeemed nation, and made an heir of the everlasting covenants. God had said unto this people,

> For you are a holy people unto the Lord your God; The Lord your God has chosen you to be a special people unto himself, above all people who are upon the face of the earth. (Deut. 7:6)

Israel occupies a place of blessing that no other nation has come close to possessing. They may be out of favor today and under God's hand of discipline, but they are still the nation God called "the apple of His eye." Only the Church, made up of those whom the Holy Spirit indwells, has a place of greater blessing than national Israel.

> For I could wish that I myself were accursed from Christ for my brethren, my kinsmen according to the flesh, who are Israelites; to whom pertains the adoption, and the glory, and the covenants, *and the giving of the law,* and the service of God, and the promises; whose are the fa-

thers, and of whom, as concerning the flesh, Christ came, who is over all, God blessed forever. Amen. (Rom. 9:3–5)

The New Testament throws some light on this hard-to-conceive truth when it says the law was "added because of transgression" (Gal. 3:19). Whatever divine ruling was extant before Moses was evidently retained to a large degree, and to this the Mosaic Law was added. Abraham had some understanding of divine requirements, for the Old Testament says of him, "Because Abraham obeyed Me and kept My charge, My commandments, My statutes and My laws" (Gen. 26:5). This appears to be a four-fold division of the will of God for men of Abraham's time. Whether it was oral or written, there seems to be no doubt that men were well aware of its requirements; and so there is no place for excuse.

There is some evidence that a written book, or books, containing the words of God circulated among the Jews before the Old Testament material that is in our possession today. Israel may well have had a Bible that is no longer extant, or needed, in the light of accepted Scripture as presented to the Church since the present age began. The Old Testament refers to a number of books that are unknown now but were at one time considered Scripture. These include references to the Book of Jasher (Josh. 10:13), the Book of Nathan, (2 Chron. 36:8), the Book of Shemaiah, (2 Chron. 12:15) and the Book of records (Ezra 4:15).

God has spoken at different times to men who were undergoing severe trials, and the message was always the same: "Be ye holy; for I am holy" (Lev. 11:44). This is an inherent responsibility for all men. The Bible leaves little

God's Plan for the Ages

room for the unbeliever to maneuver about in his excuses. The New Testament says,

> For the wrath of God is revealed from heaven against *all* ungodliness and unrighteousness of men, who suppress the truth in unrighteousness, because that which is known about God is evident *within* them; for God made it evident to them. For since the creation of the world His invisible attributes, His eternal power and divine nature, have been clearly seen, being understood through what has been made, so that they are *without excuse*. (Rom. 1:18–20, italics added)

Inherent responsibility differs from the Mosaic Law system, in that the system promises recognition in the form of blessings that are not otherwise available to those who comply with its terms. In comparison, inherent law is that to which the creature is inseparably related by creation. This principle has been adequately illustrated in the review of the first three covenants, as seen in this study.

The Mosaic Covenant is composed of three major parts, all of equal importance. Through the intervening years since Moses' time, one part only, the moral law—consisting of the Ten Commandments—has been stressed by men above the others. This fact alone has caused a considerable amount of confusion, especially in the Church. The Mosaic covenant in its total coverage is:

1. The Moral Law (Exod. 20:1–17): the Ten Commandments
2. The Civil Law (Exod. 21:1–23:13): regulations for the conduct of society among the Israelites. Most civil law of Western nations is based on this code

3. The Ceremonial Law (Exod. 23:14–31:18): governing the offerings and sacrifice in the service of worship of Jehovah

These three parts comprise the Mosaic Law. Israel was obligated to abide by all three. Some Gentiles believe and teach that one must keep the law in this the Church Age, but they pick and choose which portions they apply to themselves. Almost always they limit the parts they apply to the moral and civil sections, and even here they prove to be selective by ignoring some things entirely. An example of this selective procedure is seen in the lack of enforcement of capital punishment (see Exod. 21:12). This process is a moot issue today—in the light of the fact that the Mosaic law was directed to Israel only, and the Gentiles have never been under this law, as such. This is not to say the Gentiles are not under the principle of law, but they are not part of the covenant God made with Israel through Moses.

The imposition of law did not change the old sin nature. It was the character of personal wrongdoing that was changed. The change was from "sin that is not imputed where there is no law" (Rom. 5:13), to sin that is rebellion against the known command of God.

> For until the law sin was in the world; but sin is not imputed when there is no law. Nevertheless, death reigned from Adam to Moses, even over them that had not sinned after the similitude of Adam's transgression . . . (Rom. 5:13–14)

> But sin, that it might appear sin, working death in me by that which is good—that sin by the commandment [law] might become exceedingly sinful. (Rom. 7:13)

The giving of the law did not result in an obedient people, but rather it proved their sinfulness and their inability to produce righteousness. The natural man cannot, by his own effort, make himself acceptable to God.

> Not by works of righteousness which we have done, but according to his mercy he saved us, by the washing of regeneration, and renewing of the Holy Spirit. (Titus 3:5)

The law was only effective as it drove the transgressor to Christ. "I do not make void the grace of God; for if righteousness come by the law, then Christ is dead in vain." (Gal. 2:21)

THE PALESTINIAN COVENANT

The second of the three covenants God made with Israel during the fifth dispensation was also made and recorded through Moses. It is called the Palestinian Covenant, because it covers the occupation of the Promised Land by the Israelites revealed in Deuteronomy 30. The Abrahamic Covenant guaranteed Israel a land of their own, but this covenant sets the conditions under which the nation will occupy that land. There is a sense in which the Abrahamic Covenant was addressed to one man and his immediate family, which included his son and grandson. The Palastinian Covenant not only reiterates but also broadens the original covenant and applies it to the extended family, the entire nation of Israel.

The Palestinian Covenant contains seven components. These seven items picture the history of the nation Israel until they are safely in the land that God has promised under His blessing. The seven sections of the covenant as seen in Deuteronomy are:

1. Worldwide dispersion of the nation because of disobedience (v.1)
2. National repentance, with its resultant obedience (v. 2)
3. The return of the Lord and the regathering of the nation (v. 3)
4. Restoration of Israel to the Promised Land (v. 4–5)
5. National conversion (v. 6)
6. Judgment upon all Israel's enemies (v. 7)
7. Israel in the land, blessed and in fellowship with the Lord (v. 9)

All but the first of these items remain as unfulfilled until after the Church Age; therefore they fall into the category of *prophecy*. No less than eight times in this covenant is the subject of God's "I will" mentioned; that makes the events covered by this covenant just as sure and secure as is the Word of God.

THE DAVIDIC COVENANT

About five hundred yeas after the institution of the Abrahamic Covenant, God revised it for the second time with an addition that concerned His servant King David. As the original covenant was instigated by the faith of one man, Abraham, whom God called "my friend" (Isa. 41:8), so this second revision was also brought about by the faith of one man, David, whom the Scriptures declare to be "a man after God's own heart" (Acts 13:22). The additions are found in 2 Samuel 7:8–17 and are called the Davidic Covenant. The stipulations now made to the original covenant, which only made provision for a people (family) and their ownership of a particular parcel of land, embraces three new areas:

1. The house (family) of David, which would be established forever. The coming of Jesus, the Messiah, literally fulfilled this provision
2. A throne forever: the visible sign of royal authority. Jesus will occupy this throne in the future Messianic kingdom
3. A kingdom forever: the Messianic kingdom

The present study shows there are three covenants that have been established in the period of the fifth age. Two of them have been shown to be of the unconditional variety, and the remaining one is found to be very unique in that it stands alone as being conditional. Any and every attempt by men to mix or join the lone covenant with the others will only lead to error and confusion. The two unconditional covenants of the fifth age are natural complements to the unconditional covenant installed in the fourth age.

The Abrahamic Covenant, along with its two additions or extensions, the Palestinian and the Davidic Covenants, is said to be everlasting in its application. In all phases of this extended covenant, God said many different times "I will" do this and this. There were no conditions attached for men to fulfill before God would act. In strong contrast, and not to be confused with the foregoing, the Mosaic Covenant established man's responsibility during the fifth dispensation. This is the covenant that said *if* man would obey the law, then God would respond by blessing the people and the land, and they would prosper. Because this covenant required corresponding action from both parties involved, it is a conditional covenant pure and simple; it depends upon the response of men to become fully activated.

The Revelation of God

It was during the stirring events of this age God was able to reveal Himself as Lord (Jehovah), which is His redemptive name. Until this time the patriarchs knew God only as *El Shaddai*, which when translated into English as in the Authorized Version is "Almighty God". This can be a source of confusion because the word *shadd*, which is the root word of *shaddai*, is the Hebrew word for the female breast. Thus, if this name had been translated as "the Strength Giver" or even as "the Nourisher" it would have given a more accurate insight into the character of God revealed through this story.

There are other names of God that adequately express the attribute of strength or might, such as *El Gibor*, "Mighty God." The patriarchs found that God would sustain and provide for them in every circumstance.

> And God said unto Moses, "I AM THAT I AM": and he said, "Thus shall you say unto the children of Israel, I AM has sent me unto you." (Exod. 3:14).

> And God spoke unto Moses, and said unto him, "I am the LORD; And I appeared unto Abraham, unto Isaac, and unto Jacob, by the name of God Almighty [El Shaddai], but by my name Jehovah was I not known to them." (Exod. 6:3)

As the revelation of God is progressive throughout the Old Testament, God deemed the time and place was proper for further exposure of His character. When God addressed Moses in Exodus 3, He called Himself *I Am,* which is the English translation of the word known in our time as "Jehovah". This name appears in the Authorized Version as Lord, spelled in small-capital letters. To further enhance the meaning of the name Jehovah, the great *I Am*, the name carries the connotation of the "Self-existent One Who Reveals Himself." This is the name by which God is known in all His redemptive work in His relations with man. The meaning of the name is given in Exodus for the first time as God intervenes and saves His people Israel from bondage under the brutal slavery at the hand of the Egyptians.

The ten plagues by which God judged Egypt were very impressive pictures of His omnipotence and His ability to enforce His will and His word against the jurisdiction of any man. Egypt was the most powerful and feared nation on earth at this time. No king or man dared to oppose the Pharaoh of Egypt. But the Bible says, "God is no respecter of persons" (Rom. 2:11); and when Pharaoh's harsh treatment of Israel reached a peak, God intervened. The judgment of the ten plagues was the immediate result. The tenth and last of these judgments embraced both blood and death. All men (families) in Egypt suddenly realized they had a profound choice to make and they had to make it right away. There was to be either sacrificial blood sprinkled outside on the lintel and side posts of the door of their home, or there would be death on the inside that touched the firstborn of both man and beast. The Egyptians, including their leader Pharaoh, were told of the pending event before it took place, but they refused to believe (Exod. 11:1–

10). The Israelites, for the most part, believed and applied the blood of a lamb as instructed, and death did not touch their homes. There was great tragedy and mourning among the Egyptians that night—all because of unbelief.

This episode has become the leading illustration of the doctrine of redemption in the Bible. It was at this time that God began to reveal Himself as LORD and unfold His great plan of redemption for fallen man. It really doesn't matter in which dispensation a man lives, but that the spiritual maxim holds true: ". . . without the shedding of blood there is no remission [of sin]" (Heb. 9:22). In this instance, remission is not synonymous with forgiveness, for *sin is never forgiven*. Sin is a state of being in which men are born. It is a first-principle cause, of which sin is the inevitable effect. Men do not become sinners because of the sins they commit, but they do the things they do because of what they are. The Bible teaches that *sins* may be forgiven by the act of confession, but not *sin*. The only antidote for sin is death, either ours or Christ's death—as a substitute in our place.

Remission means "to void" or to "nullify," and it leaves an empty space. When a man accepts Jesus as Savior he experiences the remission of sin. The void produced is immediately filled by the presence of the Holy Spirit, who then begins the production of the fruit of the Spirit (Gal. 5:22–23). Sins are forgiven in the case of a believer who obeys the instructions given in 1 John 1:9, and who sincerely confesses his iniquities. The Bible clearly says "the wages of sin is death" and there is no alternative (Rom. 6:23). Just as it was in Egypt long ago, men of this age and generation also have a choice to make. They must either believe God and accept Jesus' substitutionary death and spilled blood as their own and be saved, or they may reject the Word and thus give up their own lives in a salute to stubborn pride.

It was during their flight from Egypt that the people of Israel were exposed for the first time to the *Shekinah* glory of God. It was through the medium of a pillar of cloud by day and of fire by night that God chose to reveal His presence among this people.

> And the LORD went before them by day in a pillar of a cloud, to lead them the way; and by night in a pillar of fire, to give them light; to go by day and night: He took not away the pillar of the cloud by day, nor the pillar of fire by night, from before the people. (Exod. 13:21–22)
>
> And on the day that the tabernacle was reared up the cloud covered the tabernacle, . . . and at evening there was upon the tabernacle, as it were, the appearance of fire, until the morning. So it was always: the cloud covered it by day, and the appearance of fire by night. (Num. 9:15–16)

The Shekinah stayed with Israel from the time of Moses until the time of Ezekiel, a period of between seven and eight hundred years. It finally departed from Israel in an unprecedented time of moral decadence and estrangement from God, as the nation entered a period of severe chastisement and judgment. While the *Shekinah* was in their midst, it allowed the people to get just so close to the revealed presence of God and no closer. God appeared in a thick cloud. To the average Israelite He was unapproachable. "And the LORD said unto Moses, 'Lo, I come unto you in a thick cloud, that the people may hear when I speak with you, and believe you forever" (Exod. 19:9). Only the high

The Fifth Dispensation

priest—and he but once each year—could approach the presence of the Holy God and live. The individual Israelite could only approach God through the ministry of his representative priest.

What a difference the believer experiences in the present age. As born-again ones we have the Holy Spirit dwelling within us. We are new creatures (or new creations) and have become part of the body, of which Christ is the head. The world of men has never before seen a creature such as what God has made of each individual Christian. Now the believer has Jesus as his High Priest, and He has opened the way into the very presence of the Father for us. "We are accepted [by the Father] in the Beloved" (Eph. 1:6). To the Israelite of old, God was seen as so holy and so fearful that the people wanted no direct contact with Him, not even to have Him talk with them.

> And all the people saw the thunderings, and the lightenings, and the noise of the trumpet, and the mountain smoking; and when the people saw it, they moved, and stood afar off. And they said unto Moses, "You speak with us, and we will hear; but do not let God speak with us, lest we die." And Moses said unto the people, "Fear not; . . ." And the people stood afar off, . . . (Exod. 20:18–20*a*)

THE CLOSE OF THE FIFTH DISPENSATION

Each of the former ages ended with the failure of men to live according to the situations that God outlined for them. Thus they did not attain the righteousness that God demanded for fellowship with Himself. The efforts of man in this fifth age proved to be no exception, and the age ends in an appalling failure of man. From the beginning there was a horrifying succession of mistakes and failures. Each led to an ever-increasing severity of judgment, with the worst of these as still being a future event. While the people were yet encamped before Mt. Sinai they constructed an idol, a golden calf, and fell to worshiping it instead of God. For this, 3,000 Israelites were slain (Exod. 32:28). Many years later, after Israel had again sinned grievously against the Lord, the nation was overpowered and made captive by their enemy, the neighboring nation of Assyria.

> For so it was, that the children of Israel had sinned against the LORD their God. . . . And they did secretly those things that were not right . . . they set up images and idols in every high hill, . . . and there they burned incense, . . . and wrought wicked things to provoke the LORD to anger; for they served idols, of which the LORD had said unto them, "You shall not do this thing." They rejected his statutes, and his covenant that he made with their fathers, . . . and they left all the commandments of the LORD . . . (2 Kings. 17:7, 9–12, 15–16)

Judah failed to heed the warning of the judgment against the northern nation, Israel; and they in their turn, having likewise failed to keep the law, succumbed to their enemies the Chaldeans (Babylonians) in 606 B.C., about two centuries after Israel's fall.

> Zedekiah, . . . did that which was evil in the sight of the LORD, . . . he hardened his heart from turning unto the LORD. Moreover, all the chief of the priests, and the people, transgressed very much after all the abominations of the nations, and polluted the house of the LORD. They mocked the messengers of God, and despised his words, and mis-

The Fifth Dispensation

> used his prophets, until the wrath of the Lord arose against his people, till there was no remedy. Therefore, he brought upon them the king of the Chaldeans, who slew their young men with the sword, . . . And they burned the house of God. . . . And those who escaped from the sword carried he away to Babylon, . . . (2 Chron. 36:11–12, 14, 16–17, 19, 20)

It was in this manner and for this reason the Jewish people were once again made servants and slaves to Gentile nations. This marked the beginning of the Times of the Gentiles which is still in progress today. The Church Age, or the dispensation of the Church, runs its entire course within the Times of the Gentiles. In doing so it becomes an interruption of the dispensation of law. This dispensation (law) will pick up again and continue for a short period of time until its prophesied end, but this will only occur after the Church is completed and removed through the Rapture.

As time passed, history shows the Roman Empire became a world power. It was while under Roman rule that the Messiah was born and rejected by the leaders of the Jewish state. Being subject to Roman law, Israel did not have the authority to exercise capital punishment. It was upon the insistence of these Jewish leaders the local Roman authorities put Jesus on a Roman cross to die.

> You men of Israel, hear these words: Jesus of Nazareth, a man approved of God among you by miracles and wonders and signs, which God did by him in the midst of you, as you yourselves also know; Him, being delivered by the determinate counsel and foreknowledge of God, you have taken, and by wicked hands have crucified and slain; . . . (Acts 2:22–23)

A few short years after this despicable act, the Jews were badly beaten in battle because of insurrection against their Roman rulers, and the city of Jerusalem was destroyed. The Jewish people were then forcibly scattered throughout all the known world. This dispersal of the Jews into every nation of the world has been the situation for two millennia, until the year A.D. 1948, when by a United Nation's mandate Israel once again became a legitimate nation, having a homeland of their own and becoming a magnet for all Jews everywhere.

The final scenario of this fifth dispensation will be the Tribulation period, called in the Bible "the time of Jacob's trouble." The immediate cause of the Tribulation is the Jew's rejection of Jesus as their Messiah. The insertion of the Church Age has separated the cause and its effect by some two thousand years, but nevertheless, the two incidents are inseparably linked together. If one could mentally remove the Church Age and join the two parts of the Age of Law, it would be readily seen they form a continuous line of related events.

The Activity of Satan

Throughout all the ages, Satan has perpetrated and instigated anti-God activities and movements among men by using others as his agents while he himself remains hidden in the background. He is a master at deception. As a rule he uses others—the fallen angels, ungodly men, and even different events—as fronts to carry out his evil machinations. There are at least three exceptions to this rule, all three occurring in the fifth dispensation. They occur at critical points in God's plan of salvation for men. Satan recognized the im-

The Fifth Dispensation

portance of these events in regard to his own plans concerning men, so he made the decision to personally intervene.

The first of these extraordinary incidences was his attempt to derail the Lord Jesus' ministry before it fairly began. As the precursor to His ministry, Jesus, all the while fasting, was tempted by Satan for forty days. It was during this time Satan presented three different schemes to the Lord to tempt Him to abandon the will of the Father (Luke 4:1–13). Jesus, seeing through the duplicity of His antagonist, made frequent and fluid use of the Scriptures to overcome the tempter. As a result, this occasion has become an outstanding illustration to all believers, regardless of the age in which they live, of the right way to overcome temptation: by being fluent in the Word of God. "Resist the devil [temptation] and he will flee from you" (James 4:7).

The second and third time Satan made personal intervention a part of his plan in his desire to supersede the Lord, he used almost identical tactics. Not wanting to trust the more delicate parts of the work to inferior beings, his decision was to insert himself into what proved to be the critical part of his scheme. The first of these two occasions arose in the closing hours of Jesus' ministry here on planet Earth. Jesus' enemies were seeking for the proper time and means to kill Him, when Satan, seeing his opportunity, stepped into the fabricated scene. The Scripture says he entered into Judas (Luke 22:3), one of the twelve disciples, and it was from that vantage point he engineered the betrayal and arrest of Jesus. This, of course, led to Jesus' crucifixion and death. There are frequent accounts of demon possession, but this is one of the rare times the Bible speaks of someone being possessed by the devil himself. Incredible!

Through this event Satan thought betraying Jesus would wreck God's plan of salvation for fallen man. Instead, he inadvertently supplied the missing parts of God's plan, and by doing so brought the plan to full fruition. Ironically, Satan brought about his own defeat and eventual downfall. Even though Jesus died, He arose, and His resurrection spelled victory over sin and death. Satan came out of this account as the loser.

Shortly after the Rapture of the Church, which will mark the end of the Church Age, the Dispensation of the Law will once again be in force. This Dispensation of the Law will take up again at the point where it was so summarily interrupted, by the introduction of the Church Age. Israel will again be into temple worship, with the sacrifices being made and the law being taught. About this same time, the Man of Sin, who will be the head of the restored Roman government (Empire), will sign a seven-year mutual defense treaty with Israel. This is the treaty that will be broken at its midpoint (Dan. 9:27), as the forces at Rome's disposal attack Israel. It is of extreme interest to note that Satan once again is personally involved as the instigator of this treacherous action. The purpose is to destroy the Jewish people and thus make all God's promises and His word worthless. The Scripture says ". . . the Dragon [Satan] gave him [the Man of Sin] his power and his throne and great authority" (Rev. 13:2).

When the issue is of enough importance Satan is not the least bit loath to enter the fray. It has been shown how Satan involved himself in no less than three major thrusts in his attempt to unseat God as the Sovereign One.

1. He confronted Jesus in an aborted effort to curtail God's plan of salvation (Matt. 4:1–11)

2. He entered Judas and led him to betray Jesus, which led to Jesus' death (Luke 22:3–6)
3. He will join the Beast and the False Prophet to form the "unholy trinity"; and in that role he will betray Israel again and bring that people to the brink of annihilation (Matt. 24:21–22)

Satan revealed his whole desire, that which motivates him when he expressed his five "I wills" in defiance of God's will. The Bible says,

> How are you fallen from heaven, O Lucifer, son of the morning! How are you cut down to the ground, you who did weaken the nations! For you have said in your heart *I will* ascend into heaven, *I will* exalt my throne above the stars of God; *I will* sit also upon the mount of the congregation, in the sides of the north, *I will* ascend above the heights of the clouds, *I will* be like the Most High. (Isa. 14:12–15, italics added)

Satan has never varied or swerved from his program. He will singlemindedly carry on in his opposition as God's most bitter and unrelenting foe until his own crushing and fiery end.

Satan, through his associate, the Man of Sin, breaks his treaty with Israel and a state of war ensues. In this war Israel is defeated, Jerusalem is captured, and the temple is taken. In his lust for power and glory, and under the auspices of Satan, the Man of Sin will erect an idol in the holy place of the temple and demand that men worship it (Matt. 24:15). This act of defilement, coupled with his persecution of Israel—the special treasure of the Lord—brings the unadulterated wrath of God into play, and the Great Tribulation becomes a fearsome and terrible reality.

Chapter 8

The Sixth Dispensation

God was working amid the furor and distress that became so prominent during the latter part of Jesus' ministry and extended through the time of His trial, death, and resurrection. Out of the seeming chaos of the time, the Church was born. Jesus had promised that it would be so, for He had said, ". . . upon this rock I will build my church" (Matt. 16:18). The rock that He was referring to was the solid, unshakable truth contained in Peter's statement, He (Jesus) is ". . . the Christ, the Son of the living God (Matt. 16:16). The Church is built upon Christ and the finished work He accomplished in His ministry while here on earth. He said "I came to do the will of Him who sent me" (John. 4:34). If it were not for Jesus' substitutionary death, and His resurrection from the dead that followed, there would be no Church. God's plan called for the experience of regeneration, a spiritual new birth, in which all believers would be born into His family as sons and would be formed into a single corporate body infused throughout with the Holy Spirit.

God's primary purpose and attention was now directed away from Israel and the law, and centered on the Gentiles and the building of the Church. His spoken intent is to form a "glorious Church," a fit Bride for His Son—Jesus Christ. In his writing to the church at Rome, the apostle Paul worded it this way, ". . . that blindness in part is happened to Israel, until the fullness of the Gentiles come in" (Rom. 11:25). The word *until,* as it is used in this sentence, is a fascinating word. The Church is largely made up of Gentile believers, and one day—possibly soon—the last believer will be added to the Church and that body will be complete. At that time, the Church will be caught up (raptured) out of this world and the sixth dispensation will have come to an end. The Lord's attention then reverts to Israel, and the fifth dispensation will run out its course. In the meantime, the Church is still in the process of being finished. The Bible says,

> Having made known unto us the mystery of his will, according to his good pleasure which he has purposed in himself; . . . That we should be to the praise of his glory, who first trusted in Christ; in whom you also trusted after you heard the word of truth, the gospel of your salvation; in whom also after you believed, you were sealed with that Holy Spirit of promise, who is the earnest of our inheritance until the redemption of the purchased possession, unto the praise of his glory. (Eph. 1:9, 12–14)

The sixth dispensation had its beginning on that day of Pentecost that followed the Lord Jesus' ascension back to the Father in heaven. That is the day the Holy Spirit made His debut on earth and began His residential ministry in

The Sixth Dispensation

the hearts and lives of believers, which precipitated the birth of the Church. In John's Gospel, Jesus said, "Nevertheless, I tell you the truth: It is expedient for you that I go away; for if I go not away, the Comforter [Holy Spirit] will not come unto you; but if I depart, I will send him unto you" (John 16:7). Now, nearly 2,000 years later, the sixth age, which is the present age, has already shown itself to be the longest of all the dispensations. This age will end when the Church is complete and then raptured into the Lord's presence.

The responsibility of men in this dispensation is to accept the gospel of salvation, which is to believe on the Lord Jesus Christ to be saved from the penalty of sin. Every human being needs this salvation, "For all have sinned, and are falling short of the glory of God" (Rom. 3:23). The Bible declares this penalty to be condemnation and eternal separation from God.

> For God so loved the world, that he gave his only begotten Son, that whosoever believes in him should not perish, but have everlasting life. For God sent not his Son into the world to condemn the world, but that the world through him might be saved. He that believes on him is not condemned; but he that believes not *is condemned already*, because he has not believed in the name of the only begotten Son of God. And this is the condemnation, that light is come into the world, and men loved darkness rather than light, because their deeds were evil. (John 3:16–19, italics added)

As the counterpoint of separation from God, believing in Jesus Christ is to activate an instant spiritual miracle, and regeneration takes place. The one who believes is then indwelt by the Holy Spirit, and immediately he or she becomes a child of God, born into His family.

> Beloved, now are we the children of God, and it does not yet appear what we shall be, but we know that, when he shall appear, we shall be like him; for we shall see him as he is. And every man that has this hope in him purifies himself even as he is pure. (I John 3:2–3)

We are living today in the age when there is no special covenant between God and man. The Church is not a covenanted body, for Jesus arbitrarily said, "I will build my Church" (Matt. 16:18). A covenant is an agreement entered into by two or more persons. It is a solemn compact that often has legal ramifications. No such compact or covenant has ever been associated with the Church. God did not confer with men before making His decision to call out a body of believers in this age to comprise the mystical Bride for His Son. That was a decision made before the foundation of the world.

Churchmen throughout this age who have a legalistic bent in their thinking have tried to bring elements of the covenant of the last age into their teaching for the Church; and in doing so have caused much chaos. A common statement made by many church leaders of our day, either by voice or by print, is that men are saved by grace alone (which is true), but they must live by keeping the law (which is not true) to remain saved. The apostle Paul in the Book of Romans refutes the part of this teaching that is marked as untrue when he writes in a very positive manner, "Wherefore, my brethren, you are become dead to the law by the body of Christ, . . ." (Rom. 7:4). This truth is further strengthened when God, through Paul, said, "Now if we be dead with Christ, we believe we shall also live with him, . . ." (Rom. 6:8).

Not willing to bow the knee or the heart to the Almighty, many of these same men reach out blindly and drag in certain aspects of the compact that is yet to be made with Israel for the next age; thus they compound the error and cause even more chaos. Their agenda for today is a mishmash of doctrine and theology from three different ages, on which no two liberal scholars can substantially agree.

The Church is existent and growing because of the ministry and work of the Holy Spirit. Man is not central or even necessary in the propagation of this body. Man may be wondrously used of God—for we are told to go, to preach (Mark 16:15), and to pray—but this is only in conjunction with the Spirit. If the Spirit is not working in any given situation, man can do nothing and only labors in vain. In the passage of Matthew 16 Jesus said, "*I* will build *My* Church." He did *not* say "You will build My church," nor did He say, "I will build a church for you." It is really time for men to get their doctrine straight.

> And when he [the Holy Spirit] is come, he will reprove the world of sin, and of righteousness, and of judgment: of sin, because they believe not on me; of righteousness, because I go to my Father, and you see me no more; of judgment, because the prince of this world is judged. (John 16:8–11)

Men may devise many different programs and have numerous ideas on how to increase their ministry and cause outsiders to attend their meetings, but unless the Spirit of God is leading and the work is Spirit oriented, it amounts to just so much bombast.

THE COURSE OF THE AGE

The Church Age is outlined in fair and accurate detail in the Book of Revelation, chapters 2–3. These chapters reveal the history of the Church on earth, from its beginning to its tragic and abysmal end. In Revelation 1, the apostle John receives his instructions from the Lord. He is not only given the order to write, but even more implicitly, he is told the subjects on which he is to write. These instructions open three definite but limited areas for him to clarify (Rev. 1:19):

1. *The vision of the Lord he has just seen*: This vision of the Lord is described in the remaining part of chapter 1.
2. *"The things that are"*: To better understand this terse statement, one should read the things or conditions that exist during this present Church Age. These things are seen in the seven letters to the seven *representative* churches of Asia Minor, as given in chapters 2–3.
3. *"The things that shall be hereafter"*: In easier words to understand, and for clarification on this point, it should be read, "the things that will occur after this Church Age has run its course and is finished." These things are written in Revelation 4–22. All remain for future development, and at this time are strictly in the area of prophecy.

The seven churches of Asia that John was instructed to address were chosen with a definite objective in mind. That they were seven local and existing congregations there can be little doubt. It should also be recognized that these particular churches were chosen from among many that existed in the area. These seven churches were chosen by the Holy Spirit because their spiritual, or interior condition, were representative of the successive stages of Christendom throughout the course of the sixth dispensation. These churches were chosen with care, because God has a specific message He is relating to believers. The message contained is the Church Age is no different than those ages that preceded it, in that again men fail to attain righteousness apart from total dependence upon God and His Word.

The history of the Church, as revealed in Revelation, discloses that there are two great dangers always present and ready to wreak havoc in the church—if and when they gain the ascendency. Both of the dangers mentioned have similar sources, for each of them begin when some power usurps the place of Jesus as the head and authority of the Church. These twin dangers are really opposite poles of the same satanic scheme. One method starts at the top, with the clergy making the claim to be in control of the church; while the other method starts at the bottom, with the people demanding to be in control. This second danger involves the principle of majority rule. The first of these perils appeared in the beginning years of the Church. The warning of this hazard comes in the letter to the church at Ephesus.

Ephesus

The church in Ephesus (Rev. 2:1–7) is historically and spiritually representative of Christendom and all that depicted the Church in the world during the first and second century. The One who speaks is the sovereign God, and He has something for which to commend this church. His knowledge of them was complete; He knew their works, their sacrificial labors, their patience, and their hatred for Nicolaitanism—the only thing in the New Testament that it is stated God hates (Rev. 2:6). It is good for men to hate the same things that God hates.

The name *Nicolaitanes* comes from two words: *nikao,* which means "to conquer", and *laos,* which means "people." A literal translation would be to rule over the people. It is from the word *laos* that we get the word *laity*. If the word *Nicolaitanes* is used here symbolically, it would be in reference to the beginning of a so-called priestly order of the clergy, which would then divide the church into two groups: clergy and laity—with the former ruling over the latter. It is imperative that believers recognize Christ to be the head (authority) of the Church. When men devise a false leadership, there is an immediate split—a divided command—that results from confusion among the followers.

God has made provision for His Church and its local leadership right from the beginning. An early example of this is seen in Acts 13 where the church in Antioch had prophets and teachers among its leading men. An extended portion of Scripture in the Book of Ephesians tells that He has given consideration to meet all the needs that the local church may have. There it says,

> And He gave some, apostles; and some, prophets; and some, evangelists; and some, pastors and teachers for the perfecting of the saints for the work of the ministry for the edifying of the body of Christ, till we all come in the unity of the faith, and the knowledge of the Son of God. (Eph. 4:11–13)

There is no provision made for a local church to be controlled by a man, or a group of men, from outside its own

The Sixth Dispensation

local jurisdiction. Strengths of various kinds may be attained by groups banding together to meet different needs that arise, but each church should retain its own sovereignty under God. When these churches represent different tribes or different nations, and especially different cultures, there is certain to arise varied opinions on any given subject. All the leaders may think of themselves as being equal, but some will go beyond that and think of themselves as being first among equals.

It is this uncontrollable lust for religious power and authority among men that God hates, and it has its roots in the Church from the first century. When the Bible speaks of hate, especially the Lord's hate, it is speaking of an inward indignation against evil, against that which is intrinsically wrong. This is not an expression of an evil temper. The message to the Church of the first century was not that they held the doctrine of Nicolaitanism, but that they did not aggressively resist it. That which was hated yet tolerated in the first century Church soon became accepted and practiced in the Church represented by Pergamus—the Church of the fourth century. This is the message that the churches in America today should hear and heed. Indifference to evil is an insult to a holy God. The sin of the churches is a toleration of evil and of evil men. The Lord said, " . . . you have left your first love." The wording here is important. The Lord did not say the believers involved in this episode *lost* their first love, but that they *left* it. They left it behind as they went on to other things that proved to be of far less importance.

Smyrna

Not much will be said concerning this letter (Rev. 2:8–11) except to say it represents the conditions in Christendom during the third and fourth centuries. This is the time when the Church had to withstand ten periods of various degrees of persecution, most of which were at the hands of the Roman civil authorities. Smyrna contains the word *myrrh*, which is an ointment or balm used in dressing wounds. The early Church suffered much at the hands of Jewish leaders, but as it began to grow and expand outward, the persecution became more and more from Gentile sources. This was truly a suffering Church.

The Church grows under persecution, and it was in this period that the Church expanded throughout the known world. This church may have been poor in the world's estimation, but God said they were spiritually rich.

Pergamos

Where the church at Smyrna withstood pressure from without, the church at Pergamos (Rev. 2:12–17) had to face ruin from within. Historically this church represents the period of time from the fourth to the sixth centuries, when the union between church and state took place. Where persecution failed, world conformity succeeded. The marriage of church and state in the early part of the fourth century brought the two together as one, with the inevitable result that the state supports and controls the church.

A second area for rebuke opened when the Church made the decision to accept the doctrine of the Nicolaitanes. That which was hated and avoided by the first-century Church (Ephesus) has been accepted as doctrine and put into practice by this fourth-century Church. The laity thus became subservient to an entrenched clerical hierarchy. The sin of the Church was the toleration of evil, especially evil, unsaved leaders as members of the clergy.

Jesus Himself used a simple illustration in the Gospel of Matthew as an example of what is to be expected of the individual believer in his journey through this life's experiences.

> Enter in at the narrow [strait] gate; for wide is the gate, and broad is the way, that leads to destruction, and many there be who go in that way; because narrow [strait] is the gate, and hard is the way, which leads to unto life, and few there be that find it. (Matt. 7:13–14)

The King James Version of the Bible is the one that uses the word *strait* in place of the word *narrow*, and it is a far more picturesque word for the image being created. The word *strait* signifies a narrow water passage between two headlands. This verbal illustration used by the Lord is of major significance, as the believer can picture the danger involved of the clergy ruling as one headland and the people ruling as the other and both as equally destructive. Men must let the Lord guide the Church with a sure and steady hand on the wheel. He will steer a course that will avoid shipwreck and disaster. What is true for the individual, as reported by Jesus in the illustration, is equally true for the Church as a body.

Thyatira

Historically, Thyatira represents the Church of the sixth through the fifteenth centuries (Rev. 2:19–29), which is the age of the papacy. The name Thyatira is translated by some to mean "continual sacrifice," which would mean the *mass*. The mass is the very heart of Roman Catholicism. The mass denies the finished work of Christ and inevitably led to the

God's Plan for the Ages

Dark Ages and to medieval Christianity. This is the full-blown fruit of Nicolaitanism.

The One who speaks to this church is the Son of God. What a contrast—for to the Roman church, He is only the son of Mary. The text says He has "eyes like a flame of fire." He sees everything, nothing is hidden from Him. He also has "feet like fine brass." As brass typifies judgment, this One will not tolerate or close His eyes to evil. He is the omniscient God—He knows all. It is repeated twice that He knows their works, and He indicates their works are more prominent than their faith or their love.

The Lord finds it necessary to give this church a very strong rebuke, for He said He had a "few things against" them. First, He brings before them the name Jezebel, the woman who led Israel into idolatry and immorality. The inference is that those in Thyatira were walking the same ungodly path. Jesus then says He gave them time to repent, and they did not. It may be well to recognize that the Lord dealt with this church for a full millennia. The Word of God was no longer this church's authority but the word of the organized church had taken His place. The professing Church was being led away from the person of Christ into a man-devised system—from Christ to Mary, and from the cross to the mass.

The prevalence of Nicolaitanism reveals a divided Church, with two widely divergent camps. The New Testament teaches the Church to be a single organism, with Christ as the head. Each believer takes his place as a member of the body, and then the body with its many different members moves and acts as the head directs. The clergy as a ruling and controlling system over any part of the Church is man-made; and knowingly or not, it usurps the place and the authority of the Lord. Since Nicolaitanism became entrenched in the very fiber of the Church's being, it has been a constantly festering ulcer. Through the centuries this lust for power by men has caused more problems, more wars, more inhumanity against fellow men, and more divisions than all other weaknesses combined. Each church prelate has a tendency to claim more power or authority than any one else in his zone of operation.

Sardis
Sardis means "a remnant," and historically it represents the Church of the fifteenth through the seventeenth centuries (Rev. 3:1–6)—Church of the Reformation. This Church period resulted as a strong backlash to the conditions existing under Thyatira, the Church of the papacy. That a change was desirable, even mandatory, is widely recognized, for the Church in general had gradually declined away from God until true faith could hardly be found.

Action in the Church is commendable, for the Church is instructed to go, to pray, to make disciples, and above all to witness to the power of the resurrected Lord. On the other side of the equation, reaction to an existing situation is almost always detrimental; the church of Sardis represents reaction at its worst.

The One who speaks to this church at Sardis is the same who has the seven-fold Spirit of God, signifying He is the all-sufficient One. He is able to meet their every need. There is no room, nor necessity, for Mariolatry if they would only allow Him to occupy His rightful place as head of the Church. He holds the seven stars, which represent the testimony of the Church; apart from Him all ministry of the Church is dead works. The Lord carries a dreadful announcement to this church when He summarizes, "I know thy works, that thou hast a name that thou livest, and art dead" (Rev. 3:1). That is a terrible indictment, but it reveals the lack of spirituality in the work of the Reformation as a whole.

Protestantism arose bearing strong protest against error and corruption. However, the protest became diluted by failure to put Jesus Christ in His rightful place as head of the Church. When He is given that place, there is found no place for spiritual vacuum, nor for intrusion by men. The Reformation produced some great and honorable men, but they were still men. Most all the leaders of the Reformation were trained in the Roman Catholic church and were ordained into the priesthood by that organization. Each man was thoroughly indoctrinated in the theory of the succession of priests—supposedly going all the way back to Peter, whom the Roman church claimed to be the first pope. When these men came out of Roman Catholicism, each man carried a certain amount of Catholic baggage with him. They vied with one another for power and authority, with the inevitable result of division in the Church. Out of this bickering and turmoil came state churches, denominationalism, and a whole host of different theories of doctrinal and theological systems.

The thing that is said the Lord hated—Nicolaitanism—has been allowed to continue. Its presence is seen in the establishment of various state churches and ecclesiastical systems. Masses of people became nominally Protestant because of the region they were born in or because of the king they served. This carried-over error made it possible for individuals to be declared members of the Church because of their physical birthright or their national citizenship, rather than by regeneration—being born again.

The Sixth Dispensation

"Thou hast a name that thou livest, and art dead." The Scriptures do not say this is a dying church but one that was spiritually lifeless. The Protestant Reformation brought on lifeless profession—dead orthodoxy. Men preferred to be doctrinally correct but spiritually bankrupt, as Paul wrote to Timothy, "Having a form of Godliness, but denying the power of it; from such turn away" (2 Tim. 3:5). The battle cry of the Reformation was "justification by faith alone," but that has long since been lost to the greater part of Christendom. Faith in God's Word became a rare commodity indeed. Vast multitudes of those who call themselves Protestants do not believe in sin, or hell as a literal place. They do not believe that Jesus is God, and they do not believe He arose from the dead.

Leader competed with leader over doctrinal issues and Protestantism splintered and fractured until it was virtually unrecognizable. At best it may be said that the Reformation began well, but it quickly deteriorated into a series of religious systems that the Lord has described as being spiritually dead—lifeless. It is not a hopeless situation—praise God—for in every age, in every generation, there always remains a faithful core. The testimony of the risen Lord goes on and on. The faithful part of the Reformation believers developed into the Philadelphia church, and the rest became what is now called the Laodicean church.

Philadelphia

In all the record of church history, the church at Philadelpha alone received a message of high commendation with no rebuke (Rev. 3:7–13). The name of this church is formed from two Greek words, *phileos* and *delphia*, which means "love for a brother." When reversed in English they would be seen as "brotherly love." This church represents Christendom in the eighteenth through the twentieth centuries. God placed before this church an open door; and this age, more than any other, has been known for its missionary effort worldwide.

The faithful remnant of Sardis, called the "overcomers", will be those who are the early leaders of the Philadelphia era and will help establish direction and priorities in this most opportune time. Church history reveals at least two major revivals swept through the Western world during this age, one in each century. The tragedy of the time is that the dead orthodoxy of Sardis carried over and became the foundation blocks for the distasteful Church that will be spewed out and rejected by the Lord.

The Church Age represented by Philadelphia is unique above all others in that it is the one that received promise of escape from the time of trial (Tribulation) that is due to come on all earth dwellers. To this church alone He said, "Behold, I come quickly."

Many centuries have passed since the Church had its beginning, and the second potent danger to its existence has always remained as a threat. The two perils mentioned earlier as being present in this age represent opposite poles. The first peril, that of an organized clergy controlling the Church, raised its head in the past and caused immeasurable damage to the visible Church on earth. The second peril, that of the people controlling the Church, is now a very present danger and many local churches are suffering under that burden today. It is only because of the climate in the civil arena that the second danger has now become a major factor in these last days. Anything that displaces Jesus

Christ as the head of the Church is wrong, and the Church will suffer because of it.

Laodicea

Laodicea—the church of the last days—is the seventh and last of those assemblies chosen to portray the history of the Church on earth (Rev. 3:14–22). Historically it represents the Church of the twentieth (and twenty-first?) century. The name Laodicea itself tells a story. Made of a combination of two words, *laos* and *dicea,* it translates into the "people speak" or the "people rule." The plans and goals of this church are made to satisfy the people—not Christ. The voices of the people are the final authority, instead of the Word of God. This is democracy in full flower. It may be workable in politics or in society, even in business and commerce, but it is death in the Church. The message to the church of Philadelphia contains no rebuke; the message to the church of Laodicea contains no praise. As in the case of each of the former churches, to this one also He acknowledges He knows their spiritual condition. He calls them lukewarm—neither hot nor cold—but neutral, showing only indifference to Christ. They boast of their riches, of their independence—they have no need of anything or of anybody. This church boasts of everything but ignorance; but the Lord assesses their condition by saying they don't know their true condition, which is wretched, poor, blind, and naked. Because of their wretched condition that they refuse to recognize, the Lord says of Laodicea that He will cast them out. They disassociated themselves from Christ; He in turn refuses to recognize them as His own. Philadelphia had the Lord's promise to be delivered from trial, to be "caught up," while Laodicea receives the awful warning that they are to be "spewed out" of His mouth as being a distasteful, detestable object.

His call to Laodicea is to individual fellowship. Regardless of the overall condition of the Church, the Lord *always* has a faithful few. To these, the overcomers, He promises the right to sit with Him on His throne; this promise intimating close association with Christ in His kingdom, which is soon to follow.

The sequence of the Lord in His relationship to these churches is something to note. To Sardis He said, "hold fast till I come." To Philadelphia He said, "Behold, I come quickly." And to Laodicea His words were, "Behold, I stand at the door." There is no further reference or message to a church after Laodicea. This fact stands as evidence that Laodicea is truly the Church of the last days.

THE CLOSE OF THE DISPENSATION

Through the passing of many centuries, man has failed numerous times and in many different ways. Perhaps the one error that had the most telling effect is not recognizing the Church for what it really is: the mystical body of Christ. Men live in a world that is composed of that which is both material and physical, and they are prone to view all they see from that perspective. To most men the church is a man-made organization and it is to be used, even manipulated, like any other worldly organization, to fit their personal needs of the moment. The idea that the Church is an organism enlivened by the Holy Spirit is a totally foreign concept to their thinking. Even among young believers, babes in Christ, there is a sharp lack of the discipline that leads to

The Sixth Dispensation

Bible reading, good teaching, sound doctrine—the very things that are conducive to spiritual growth. The apostle Paul wrote,

> And I, brethren, could not speak unto you as unto spiritual, but as unto carnal, even as unto babes in Christ. I have fed you with milk, and not with solid food; for to this time you were not able to bear it, neither yet now are you able. For you are yet carnal; for whereas there is among you envying, and strife, and divisions, are you not carnal, and walk as men? (1 Cor. 3:1–3)

One of the key elements of the above quoted passage is the statement by Paul that he had to feed these believers with milk. The inference being they did not feed on the Word themselves.

In the final years of the sixth dispensation, the visible Church on earth is being wracked by strife and division, most of which comes from within. The two perils spoken of previously in this chapter have, by this time, clutched the Church on earth firmly in their grip. Large segments of the Church are under the control of an established clergy, the very system the Scripture says the Lord hates (Rev. 2:6). This is the system that is known by the name of Nicolaitanism. These various systems of clergy always seem to be self-perpetuating, and they tend to embrace men who are unregenerate and who do not know Christ.

> But there were false prophets also among the people, even as there shall be false teachers among you, who secretly shall bring in destructive heresies, even denying the Lord that bought them, and bring upon themselves swift destruction. And many shall follow their pernicious ways,

> by reason of whom the way of truth shall be evil spoken of. And through covetousness shall they, with feigned [false] words, make merchandise of you. . . . For when they speak great swelling words of vanity, they allure through the lusts of the flesh, . . . those that are just escaping from them who live in error. While they promise them liberty, they themselves are the servants of corruption; . . ." (2 Pet. 2:1–3, 18–19)

> For many deceivers are entered into the world, who confess not that Jesus Christ came in the flesh. This is a deceiver and an Antichrist. (2 John 7)

Thus it has developed into a spiritual predicament of the blind leading the blind.

There are yet other large segments of the visible Church in which it is the people themselves who have seized the authority. This is a case where the people are enthralled with the thought of democracy and they insist on majority rule. Here is seen in the latter Church, just as had been prophesied, Laodicea in full flower.

> This know, also, that in the last days perilous times shall come. For men shall be lovers of their own selves, . . . having a form of godliness, but denying the power of it; from such turn away. . . . For the time will come when they will not endure sound doctrine but, after their own lusts, shall they heap to themselves teachers, having itching ears; and they shall turn away their ears from the truth, and shall be turned unto fables. (2 Tim. 3:1–2, 5, 7; 4:3–4)

Between these two Satan-inspired evils the Lord is no longer recognized as the head of the Church. His place has

The Sixth Dispensation

been seized by men. There is a very noticeable downward trend in the activity and beliefs of the Church in what is believed by many to be the closing years of this age. A plethora of false teachers leads to a large contingent of carnal believers. It is of little wonder the Lord finds this to be a lukewarm Church at best. Continuing in its ever downward spiral, the Church in the world is exhibiting a fast-developing apostasy as it approaches the time it will be willing to accept the Antichrist.

The Judgment That Follows

The spiritual condition of the Church, in the world as a whole, is in a deplorable state:

> I know your works, that you are neither cold or hot; I would you were cold or hot. So, then, because you are lukewarm, and neither cold nor hot, I will spew you out of my mouth. (Rev. 3:15–16)

This is tantamount to being absolutely indifferent to the Lord. Christendom has become so self-deluded by its seeming success, it feels as if it has need of nothing. Just as it was in all the preceding dispensations, men feel they do not need God; they can attain to righteousness on their own. It is at this point that our longsuffering God takes positive action in two interrelated directions. With these moves He closes the curtain on the scene of the sixth dispensation, the Church Age.

The first of these moves is the Rapture (catching away) of all who are truly regenerate, up from the earth and into His presence. At the end of the age there will be a small remnant of "overcomers" still living and awaiting His coming. The apostle Paul put it this way when he wrote to the Thessalonian believers, "Then we who are alive and remain shall be caught up together with them in the clouds, to meet the Lord in the air; and so shall we ever be with the Lord" (1 Thess. 4:17). The living saints of that generation will be caught up along with the many millions of others from the past 2,000 years, who will experience resurrection out from among the dead. For the first time the Church will be whole, complete, glorified, and ready to meet the Bridegroom.

At the time these wonderful and marvelous things are happening to the Bride of Christ, the true Church, the indifferent and lukewarm Church on earth will be spewed out and cast aside by the Lord—the One they have spurned as unneeded. This is a most amazing event for the human mind to grasp: the professing Church on earth rejected by the Lord as being unprofitable. This hour completes the prophecy Jesus uttered when speaking to the people, "Many will say to me in that day, 'Lord, Lord, have we not prophesied in your name? And in your name have cast out demons? And in your name done many wonderful works?' And then will I profess unto them, 'I never knew you; depart from me, you that work iniquity'" (Matt. 7:22–23). Having missed out on the Rapture, their fate becomes fearful indeed: All they have to look forward to is the multiple disasters of the Great Tribulation.

Direct Dealings with God

For the entire period of the Church Age the individual believer has a direct person-to-person relationship with God. Conversion in the human heart, in this age, is always accompanied by regeneration—the Holy Spirit comes into the person to indwell and abide there.

> And I will pray the Father, and He shall give you another Comforter, that He may abide with you forever; even the Spirit of truth, whom the world cannot receive, because it sees Him not, neither knows Him; but you know Him; for He dwells with you, and shall be in you. I will not leave you comfortless; . . . (John 14:16–18)

The truly regenerate part of the Church on earth may at all times be in the minority, but they are called the overcomers, the children of God. The Bible says of them,

> The Spirit Himself bears witness with our spirit, that we are the children of God; and if children, then heirs—heirs of God, and joint heirs with Christ—if so be that we suffer with Him, that we may be also glorified together. (Rom. 8:16–17)

Because we are children, the ear of the Father is always tuned toward us, and we can talk to Him at any time. We can talk to Him through prayer; He talks to us through the Word. It is this open communication that makes the Christian experience such a blessing. No other believers of any age have the relationship, the blessing, the hope, or the future that belongs to the Church—the Bride of Christ.

Chapter 9

The Seventh Dispensation

The seventh dispensation is the final one of the series God has predetermined for the trials of mankind in the test for righteousness. This seventh age, yet future, will begin when Christ makes His second appearance on the earth and will continue until the Great White Throne Judgment takes place. The elapsed time between these two events is reported to be one thousand years, hence the age becomes known as the *millennium*.

This last age is the most wondrous one of all. It contains elements, conditions, and personnel that are almost beyond human imagination. Until the millennium the natural human being has been pretty much alone as an occupant of planet Earth. There has been the occasional interruption by the appearance of angels in ministry, but this is the exception rather than the norm. The earth was created as the ideal place for man; but when sin came, death followed, and the Lord deemed it necessary to curse the ground. Thus the ideal no longer existed. The millennium comes close to restoring the conditions of the original creation, except that sin and death are still present.

One of the most difficult differences for the mind to grasp is that in the millennial kingdom there will be three separate and distinct stages of human beings living together side by side. The first and most wondrous stage will consist of the Church saints, who will have returned to the earth with Jesus, their Savior and Bridegroom. These saints will be in their glorified state, living in immortal, incorruptible bodies. Physical life will be on an entirely different basis at that time, for their life will be in the Spirit and not in the blood. The new glorified body will have no blood, but each person will be like the Lord after His resurrection. In the New Testament the Church saint is called "a new creation." In the Book of 1 Corinthians it says,

> Therefore, if any man be in Christ, he is a new creature [creation]; old things are passed away; behold, all things are become new. (2 Cor. 5:17)

The world has never seen a creature like the Church saint as he will appear following the Rapture. Every believer of the sixth age has been regenerated; that is, born again from above. God Himself, in the person of the Holy Spirit, lives within each individual believer, and He is the source of spiritual life. There is real satisfaction in knowing "it is God who is working in you both to will and to do of His good pleasure" (Phil. 2:13). In the broader picture, the Holy Spirit indwells the entire Church, and through Him the Church becomes a radiant, glorious bride—one fit to stand at the side of Jesus Christ, the Bridegroom. The Scrip-

The Seventh Dispensation: The Millennial Kingdom

ture gives this picture of the Church saints as they will appear in the Kingdom Age:

> But some man will say, "How are the dead raised up? And with what body do they come?" . . . So also is the resurrection of the dead. It is sown in corruption; it is raised in incorruption. It is sown in dishonor; it is raised in glory. It is sown in weakness; it is raised in Power. It is sown a natural body; it is raised a spiritual body. There is a natural body, and there is a spiritual body. (1 Cor. 15:35, 42–44)

The careful observer at this point must note that the main subject of this passage is that of a body. The Scripture is speaking of a material, physical body that makes the recipient owner a fitting candidate for life here on earth. Prior to the creation of man, God created the earth as the perfect environment on which man was to exist and thrive. There are two requirements for a creature to be classified as human: (1) to be an earth creature and (2) to be of the genus *man*. God's intent for man was that he was to be an earth dweller, and that original intent has never been changed. This fact is seen clearly in God's dealing with Abraham in the fourth dispensation. The central part of God's promise to this man and his offspring was to own and occupy a portion of land forever. To be an earth dweller necessitates the acquisition of a physical body, one that is adapted to living on earth. This is one of the primary reasons for both the incarnation and the resurrection of the Lord in the person of Jesus Christ. One thing we always have to keep in mind is that Jesus Christ has to be a man.

As the Lord's consort, the Church will assist Him in His rule over the earth. When Jesus returns He will come in a manner similar to that in which He chose to leave this earth. He will be in a physical, immortal, and now glorified human body. Assurance of this fact is given when the Bible relates the angelic message, "You men of Galilee, why stand you gazing up into heaven? This same Jesus, who is taken up from you into heaven, shall so come in like manner as you have seen him go into heaven" (Acts 1:11). When He comes it will be to establish His kingdom. He will personally rule from Mount Zion, which is near Jerusalem, and each Church saint will be His ambassador wherever they may be assigned around the world.

A second stage of human existence found on earth during this Millennial Age will be the resurrected saints, those apart from the Church Age. These saints also will have resurrected physical bodies, but in some way not clearly revealed, they will be different from the bodies provided for the Church saints. It is very likely that these saints will resume life in normal, natural bodies, very similar to bodies we know now; but they will be minus the sin nature. They will be dependent upon the Tree of Life for their long-lasting existence. Once again, as it was in the beginning, they will have free and easy access to this wondrous source of life that God has provided. Adam did not have eternal life within himself but was dependent upon an outside source for continuous long life. Since the entrance of sin into the human race, man has been denied access to this tree. The Word of God reveals that, following the completion of the test conducted through the ages, this restriction will be lifted (see Rev. 22:1–2). Whether the saints of the Millennial Age will enjoy this blessing from the hand of God is debatable. Known for sure is that no unrepentant man will ever know what the fruit of that tree tastes like.

The Seventh Dispensation: The Millennial Kingdom

This second group is composed of the saints of both pre- and post-church times, and they will *not* have experienced regeneration, so they will not have the Holy Spirit living in them. Certainly He will be with them and upon them, and they will be known as servants of the Most High God. Among this group will be Abraham, Moses, David, Daniel, and all the rest of the Old Testament saints. Those saints were not part of the Church—the Bride of Christ. Job is the man whose testimony speaks for all here:

> For I know that my redeemer lives, and that he shall stand at the latter day upon the earth; and though after my skin worms destroy this body, yet in my flesh shall I see God, whom I shall see for myself, and my eyes shall behold, and not another; . . . (Job 19:25–27)

The Church saints are resurrected and raptured up to meet the Lord before the Tribulation begins. This second company of His saints is not resurrected until after the Lord returns to the earth with His bride, the Church, to begin the millennium. Among this group will be all those saints who were martyred for their faith during the Tribulation.

There is yet another group of humans whose presence is to be noted as living during the days of the millennium. There will be some natural, living humans who will survive all the rigors and dangers of the Tribulation period, as well as the two divine judgments that closely follow that extremely trying time. This group is within itself divided into two subdivisions: Jews and Gentiles. All within this main body, including both subdivisions, are in the same state of being as are natural men living today. They still possess natural, physical, mortal human bodies—*mortal* because they will still retain their old, fallen nature. This means they must rely on Jesus Christ for salvation. The Jews of this company will be treated as a separate assemblage because of their unique experience at the hands of God.

The Jews in the Millennium

When the Lord's feet touch the earth in His Second Coming, He sets off a series of events that are the subject of much Old Testament prophecy. He first comes to the Mount of Olives, and that mountain is cleft. A great new valley is formed between the two halves of the mountain, and the topography of Israel is forever changed. This prophecy is found in the Book of Zechariah, where it says:

> And in that day His feet will stand on the Mount of Olives—and the Mount of Olives will be split in the middle from east to west by a very large valley, so that half of the mountain will move toward the north and the other half toward the south. (Zech.14:4)

The valley, thus miraculously formed, becomes the scene of some of the most spectacular events in the colorful history of the human race. It is in this valley that the final disposition of the nations of the world is decided. The Lord has prophesied, "I will gather all the nations, And bring them down to the valley of Jehoshaphat. Then I will enter into judgment with them there on behalf of My people and My inheritance, Israel, whom they have scattered among the nations" (Joel 3:2). Cartographers have for years been attempting to locate or identify the valley named here as Jehoshaphat, but with no success. There is an easy expla-

The Seventh Dispensation: The Millennial Kingdom

nation for this failure, as the valley has not as yet been formed; it remains for future revelation, as God proceeds to fulfill all that He has promised in the prophetic schedule. The prophet Joel further prophesied, "Multitudes, multitudes in the valley of decision! For the day of the Lord is near in the valley of decision" (Joel 3:14).

In chapter 12 of the Book of Daniel, in the last three verses, there are several periods of days mentioned. The days numbered here amount to seventy-five or the equivalent of two-and-one-half months. This total is the sum of two separate periods: one of thirty days, and the other of forty-five days. The total of seventy-five days seems to indicate the time to be elapsed between the close of the Great Tribulation period and the beginning of the Millennial Kingdom and the reign of Christ. Many teach that this seventy-five day period is the time of the two great judgments that take place in the "valley of decision." The first thirty days are the days of the regathering of Israel and their confrontation by the Lord. Following the judgment of Israel, the second period of days, numbering forty-five, will allow for the judgment of the nations as described in Matthew 25:31–46.

The name Jehoshaphat means "Jehovah judges," and this newly opened valley just east of the city of Jerusalem seems to bear an accurate cognomen. It is into this valley that the remnant of Israel will flee, hoping to find surcease from the horrible events that have overtaken that people, and especially that nation, in the seven years of the Tribulation period. Many have taught that the pink, or rose-colored, city and the valley of Petra in Arabia would be the place of refuge Israel would seek. A close analysis of the situation reveals the valley of Jehoshaphat fits much closer to the definition the Scripture relates to the place, the events that transpire there, and the time in which it all takes place. The remnant of Israel will flee to this valley. It is there they are confronted face to face with the Messiah they rejected and so foully abused in His first advent among them.

The judgments that take place in the valley of Jehoshaphat are on earth and are of living nations, or more specifically, of living people only. There is no resurrection involved with the judgments of this time; although there will be a regathering of the people of Israel from wherever they are scattered throughout all the nations of the world. Ezekiel prophesied of this issue when he described the events connected to the Second Coming of the Lord. He wrote:

> "As I live," declares the Lord God, "surely with a mighty hand and with an outstretched arm and with wrath poured out, I shall be king over you. And I shall bring you out from the peoples and gather you from the lands where you are scattered, . . . and I shall bring you into the wilderness of the peoples, and there I shall enter into judgment with you face to face. . . . As a soothing aroma I shall accept you, when I bring you out from the peoples and gather you from the lands where you are scattered; and I shall prove Myself holy among you in the sight of the nations. And you will know that I am the Lord, when I bring you into the land of Israel, into the land which I swore to give to your forefathers." (Ezek. 20:33–35, 41–42, NASB)

When the Lord confronts Israel in the valley of decision, He will still be bearing the wounds in His body that He suffered in the events surrounding Calvary. Due to these wounds He is easily and quickly recognized by this people. With this recognition of His person will also come the recognition of the enormity of the error they committed when

The Seventh Dispensation: The Millennial Kingdom

they rejected Him and sentenced Him to die. Great is the remorse and sorrow of this people as they become enlightened and perceive the truth. Zechariah writes of this hour and says,

> And I will pour out on the house of David and on the inhabitants of Jerusalem the Spirit of grace and of supplication, so that they will look on Me whom they have pierced; and they will mourn for Him, as one mourns for an only son, and they will weep bitterly over Him, like the bitter weeping over a first-born. In that day there will be great mourning in Jerusalem. . . . And the land will mourn, every family by itself; . . . (Zech. 12:10–11a, 12a)

This is truly a defining moment, a time of transition in the lives and the existence of the people of the nation Israel. With the recognition that this One confronting them is Jesus, and also that He is their Messiah, they are filled with deep remorse in remembrance of their past actions against Him. Israel, while in the valley of decision, finds it a fearsome and disturbing time of judgment and separation. Ezekiel prophesied of the various results that would be the outcome of this troubled time. He said,

> As I live, saith the LORD God, . . . I will bring you out from the peoples, and will gather you out of the countries in which you are scattered, with a mighty hand, and with an outstretched arm, and with fury poured out. . . . As I entered into judgment with your fathers in the wilderness of the land of Egypt, so will I enter into judgment with you, saith the Lord god. And I will cause you to pass under the rod, and I will bring you into the bond of the covenant. And I will purge out from among you the rebels, and them that transgress

against me; . . . and you shall know that I am the LORD. (Ezek. 20:33*a*, 34, 37–38*a*)

The judgment of Israel results in only one-third of the nation being refined and brought through the fire of God's wrath. Two-thirds of the people will be cut off and die. The prophecy of Zechariah tells of this time of refinement:

> And it shall come to pass that in all the land, says the Lord, two parts in it shall be cut off and die; but the third part shall be left in it. And I will bring the third part through the fire, and will refine them as silver is refined, and will test them as gold is tested; they shall call on my name, and I will hear them, I will say, It is my people; and they shall say, The LORD is my God. (Zech. 13:8–9)

The one-third part of Israel that is purified will be saved, and the word *saved* has a double meaning. They will be saved physically to go alive into the Millennial Kingdom as subjects of the King. They will also be spiritually saved, as they will be in a right relationship with the Lord. This third part of the people will constitute "all Israel" as it appears in Romans 11:26–27, reads:

> And so all Israel shall be saved; as it is written, "There shall come out of Zion the Deliverer, and shall turn away ungodliness from Jacob. For this is my covenant unto them, when I shall take away their sins.

This passage, along with the quoted passage above from Ezekiel 30 speaks of bringing Israel into the bond of the covenant. The Book of Hebrews says, "He [Jesus] is the mediator of a better covenant, which was established upon

The Seventh Dispensation: The Millennial Kingdom

better promises" (Heb. 8:6). The old, conditional Mosaic Covenant proved to be unworkable because of the weakness and sinfulness of the people who were party to it. God had prophesied there would be another covenant made with Israel.

Israel's Responsibility

Israel's responsibility in the seventh dispensation will be to *do* the law and be an example of godly living and of righteousness to all the nations. This was God's purpose for Israel from the moment He chose Abraham. Abraham's descendants through Isaac were to be, and will be, the witnesses of the living God to all the nations. In the Millennial Kingdom, with the Lord seated on David's throne and ruling over all the earth, Israel will be the first among the nations. Matthew in the New Testament says of this time:

> . . . at the renewal of all things, when the Son of Man sits on His glorious throne, . . . many who are first will be last, and many who are last will be first. (Matt. 19a, 30)

This little nation that is so despised, hated, and troubled in the sixth age will be honored and looked up to in the age to come. The Gentile nations will be blessed as they come to the Jews for knowledge and instruction in worshiping the Lord God. The requirements to do the law in the kingdom will be far greater than they were in the past, when Israel tried to get by on the mere rote application to the letter of the law. In Matthew's Gospel, chapters 4 and 5 relate the very core of kingdom teaching. Here it is said:

> You have heard that it was said by them of old [law], You shall not commit adultery; but I say unto you that who-

soever looks on a woman to lust after her has committed adultery with her already in his heart. (Matt. 5:27–28)

This is kingdom teaching and graphically illustrates the far greater responsibility placed on the Jews. In the kingdom period, under the reign of Christ, the *intent* of the law will be stressed far above the letter of the law. This is part of the kingdom law that will be written in their hearts, under the auspices of the new covenant.

A new covenant will be made with Israel—who at that time will be the leading nation, and who will have the newly returned Lord seated and ruling from David's throne. The whole world will be governed from Jerusalem. The prophet Isaiah wrote,

> And it shall come to pass in the last days, that the mountain [government] of the Lord's house shall be established in the top of the mountains [governments], and shall be exalted above the hills; and all nations shall flow into it. And many people shall go and say, "Come you, and let us go up to the mountain of the Lord, to the house of the God of Jacob; and he will teach us of his ways, and we will walk in his paths; for out of Zion shall go forth the law, and the word of the Lord from Jerusalem." (Isa. 2:2–3)

THE NEW COVENANT

The three unconditional covenants made with Israel in past ages—the Abrahamic, the Palestinian, and the Davidic—all rest on the faithfulness of God alone. They are unbreakable by men and thus are eternal in nature and endurance. The one conditional covenant that was made—

The Seventh Dispensation: The Millennial Kingdom

the Mosaic Covenant—which is a law covenant, was broken and shattered by Israel and has become of no effect. The new covenant that God will make with that people will supersede the conditional covenant of the law; and it will be, in effect, an unconditional covenant. Just like the three unconditional covenants of the past, God says, "*I will* do these things." This new covenant will not depend upon Israel's conduct for continual ratification, but will depend only upon the love and faithfulness of the living Lord. The prophetic word reads,

> Behold, the days come, saith the Lord, that *I will* make a new covenant with the house of Israel, and with the house of Judah, not according to the covenant that I made with their fathers in the day that I took them by the hand to bring them out of the land of Egypt, which, my covenant *they* broke, although I was a husband unto them, saith the Lord; but this shall be the covenant that *I will* make with the house of Israel: After those days, saith the Lord, *I will* put my law in their inward parts, and write it in their hearts, and *will* be their God, and they shall be my people. And they shall teach no more every man his neighbor, and every man his brother, saying, "Know the Lord," for they shall all know me, from the least of them to the greatest of them, saith the Lord; for *I will* forgive their iniquity, and *I will* remember their sin no more. (Jer. 31:31–34, italics added)

The new covenant is made with Israel alone and is an unconditional covenant. Not less than five times God said *I will* in this covenant. Not once is His promise based on a reciprocal action on the part of Israel. The new covenant, like the three unconditional covenants that preceded it, is based only on the faithfulness of God, and magnifies His attributes of mercy and grace—mercy in that He doesn't treat Israel as they deserve; grace in that He does give to Israel that which they do not deserve. His action is nearly identical to His reception of the believer in the Church Age as He goes about His business of building the Church.

The Significant Points of the New Covenant
    I. The law will be written in their hearts.
        A. Not on exterior tablets of stone
        B. All Jews will know the Word of God
    II. God said, "I will be their God."
    III. "They shall be My people."
        A. They will not be part of the Church, the Bride
    IV. They will not have to be taught, but will all know God
    V. God said, "I will forgive your iniquity."
        A. All their sins and trespasses will be freely forgiven
    VI. "I will remember their sin no more."

The first generation of Jews who enter the Millennial Kingdom will be a saved and godly people. The 144,000 sealed Jews of Revelation 7 will almost certainly make up a large segment of this first generation of the Millennial Kingdom. Revelation 14 tells of this particular group standing with the Lord on Mount Zion after the kingdom has been inaugurated.

The second, third, and all subsequent generations will be a vastly different matter. These individuals, having been born in fleshly bodies, as were all natural men in all the past ages, will find sin is still a factor to be reckoned with.

The Seventh Dispensation: The Millennial Kingdom

There is a need for repentance and a turning to God for salvation. Just because the parents are in a right relationship with God is no guarantee the offspring will have that relationship also. There are many negative examples of this situation found in the Old Testament. Some of the most godly men in the record had descendents that were far from God and His salvation, and who refused to honor Him. The list would include Abraham himself, Aaron the high priest, Eli a priest of God, and David the king, just to name a few. What was true in ages past is equally true in the Kingdom Age—sin is pervasively present.

God is not willing that a people should perish, so He always makes a way of escape. The Kingdom Age is no different, except for the fact the people of that age have to look back to see what Jesus Christ accomplished for them in His suffering and death during His first advent on earth. During the 1000 years of the Kingdom Age there will be a millennial temple standing in Israel. The descendents of Zadok, the Levitical priest, will be the working priests (Ezek. 43:19, 44:15–31) who will make the offerings to the Lord and serve in the sanctuary. There will be sin offerings, burnt offerings, and peace offerings made during this period. These sacrifices are in no way considered to be expiatory, but rather they will be commemorative, just as the Old Testament sacrifices were anticipative. There is a close parallel here to the bread and the wine of the Lord's supper: to the believer who is "in Christ" they are physical and material symbols of a redemption already accomplished.

The Judgment of the Nations

As the judgment of Israel comes to a close in the valley of decision, the Gentile nations will be brought there, and the procedure will continue for another month and a half. The Bible says, "I will gather all nations, and I will bring them down into the Valley of Jehoshaphat, and will judge them there . . ." (Joel 3:2). The Bible reveals in the Gospel according to Matthew that a favorable verdict after this judgment of the nations will have the result that follows:

> Then shall the King say unto them on his right hand, "Come, you blessed of my Father, inherit the kingdom prepared for you from the foundation of the world." (Matt. 25:34)

The inheritance of these folks is not salvation, nor is it eternal life, for these are things that are never inherited. Rather, they inherit the right to enter the kingdom as citizens. They are not to be cut off at this time by physical death which would doom them to an eternity separated from God. They will be mortals, having all the needs that men have had in all the past ages. This would include the need for food, clothing, and shelter for the physical being; and salvation for the spiritual. In this seventh dispensation, as it was from the beginning, the human race must be sustained to carry on, so reproduction will continue in its normal day-by-day course of events. All children born to these natural parents will be born in a sinful state, just as were the offspring of all past generations. The need for repentance and conversion that leads to salvation is just as pertinent in this age as at any time in man's history. Conversion and salvation is not synonymous with regeneration. The new birth is synonymous with regeneration and is the only way in which an individual can become a member of the Body of Christ. This Body is the Church and is restricted exclusively to the sixth dispensation. At the end of the sixth dispensation, as has already been shown, the Church is complete and raptured away and will never again have any other believers added to enlarge it.

Both the first two groups of humans discussed in the Millennial Age are secure in their standing before God. They have passed from death to life and are enjoying all the blessings a loving Father and God can bestow. The believers composing these groups are living in physical, resurrected, and spiritual bodies that fit them to be in the presence of Deity, and to do so without fear.

The State of Man at the Beginning

The final dispensation begins, as did those of its predecessors, with men in fellowship with their Creator. Christ, the Prince of Peace, is firmly seated on the throne of authority and is ruling over all the earth. Daniel the prophet first told about this event centuries ago when he wrote,

> And in the days of those kings the God of heaven will set up a kingdom which will never be destroyed, and that kingdom will not be left for other people, it will crush and put an end to all these kingdoms, but it will endure forever. (Dan. 2:44)

This Kingdom Age is not to be confused with heaven itself, for sin and death still reign among natural men in this age, and there are serious matters that remain—awaiting their final disposal. However, the resurrected saints will find this age to be very near to the perfection of heaven. They will be in resurrected, immortal, and incorruptible bodies and will already have passed from death to life. It is the natural, mortal human beings with which this final age is primarily concerned.

All those natural men who enter the Millennial Kingdom as survivors of the Great Tribulation will be wearing the Mark of the Beast, either on their right hand or on their forehead. The Antichrist and his cohort, the False Prophet, have had full authority during the Tribulation, and they will have caused *all* men to receive this mark.

> And he causes all, the small and the great, and the rich and the poor, and the free men and the slaves, to be given a mark on their right hand, or on their forehead, and he provides that no one should be able to buy or to sell, except the one who has the mark, . . . (Rev. 13:16–17)

All those who enter the kingdom are not saved; some are only righteous by compulsion, and in no sense can they be termed spiritually godly. To have reluctantly accepted the Mark of the Beast as the lesser of two evils is one thing; to worship the Beast is entirely another. All men have been forced to accept the mark under the threat of death. To worship the Beast is a voluntary act and, as such, is not only against the precepts of Scripture but is an affront to the person of God. Revelation 14 twice mentions those who will suffer the wrath of God. In both instances (vv. 9, 11), these individuals are said to first of all worship the Beast, and after this it is stated they accepted his mark. It would seem that worshipping the Beast is the critical aspect of their activity and the decision on their part that condemns.

Jesus foretells of these unsaved individuals who enter the kingdom when He tells a parable in Matthew's Gospel. The subject is that of a great and royal marriage feast that is representative of the joy and blessings of the kingdom.

The Seventh Dispensation: The Millennial Kingdom

Those who were first invited to the feast have all refused to come. The king then sent out his servants with a new set of instructions. He said,

> "Go therefore to the main highways, and as many as you find there, invite to the wedding feast." And those servants went out into the streets, and gathered together *all* they found, *both evil and good*; and the wedding hall was filled with dinner guests. (Matt. 22:9–10, italics added)

There is no question that the truth being dispensed in this story is that the marriage feast, which is held in the time of the millennium, will have some guests with less than reputable character. The Scripture declares that both types of men are invited to the banquet—the evil as well as the good. *Evil* in this usage does not mean grossly wicked, but rather it means unrepentant in the heart. Jesus said, "He that is not for me is against me." Despite the lack of integrity in their hearts, these men will be forced to maintain a certain level of outward righteousness by the Lord. Any failure to do so on their part will result in quick, but just, retribution. Their actions may not present a grossly overt type of transgression, but neither are they fully committed to the Lord and to a life of righteousness. The Lord, as King over the whole earth during the millennium, demands all His subjects to adhere to a certain standard of conduct—righteousness. As long as this standard is not breached, all remains well. As soon as sin raises its head in open defiance or rebellion, it is judged swiftly and righteously; true justice is administered and continues to prevail.

Things are not so different today. As long as a man stays reasonably well within the bounds of present-day law he is usually left alone, but let him break the law and he can expect the heavy hand of authority to tap him on the shoulder and haul him into court.

Conditions within the Kingdom

With the establishment of the Millennial Kingdom the curse will be removed from the earth, and conditions will revert to being as they were prior to the Flood. The peace that comes with the Prince of Peace will extend all through nature, including the animal kingdom. Wild beasts will learn to live with one another, and there will be no slaying or bloodshed between the various species.

> The wolf and the lamb shall feed together, and the lion shall eat straw like the bullock, and dust shall be the serpents food. They shall not hurt nor destroy in all my holy mountain [kingdom], says the Lord. (Isa. 65:25)

Men shall live for long periods of time—hundreds of years—and premature death will be the result of sin. Justice will be swift and sure. The prophecy of Isaiah says of the Lord: "But with righteousness He will judge the poor, And decide with fairness for the afflicted of the earth; And He will strike the earth with the rod of His mouth, And with the breath of His lips He will slay the wicked" (Isa. 11:4). Here again is witness to the fact that there will be evil men and sinners to contend with in the millennium, and sin brings with it the punishment of death. It is no mistake or accident when the Scripture speaks of Him saying He will rule with a rod of iron.

Isaiah goes on to say that if a man dies at a hundred years of age, he dies as a child:

The Seventh Dispensation: The Millennial Kingdom

> There shall be no more in it an infant of days, nor an old man that has not filled his days; for the child will die an hundred years old, but the sinner, being an hundred years old shall be accursed. (Isa. 65:20)

Altogether this will be a time of peace, prosperity, and righteousness (Isa.11:1–9).

It is true the new covenant will be made with Israel but it is equally true that Israel will be the witness of God to all the Gentile world. This is the program that God intended when He chose Abraham centuries ago. The closing part of God's promise to that chosen man was, ". . . in you shall all families of the earth be blessed" (Gen. 12:3). Because of Israel's misconception of the person of God, as well as His overall program to include the whole world, that people failed completely in carrying out their part of the plan. They were to be His witnesses to all the nations. This part of God's promise awaits future fulfillment and provides a major reason for the new covenant. Israel will yet be God's true witness.

An Old Testament prophet said,

> Thus says the LORD of hosts: It shall yet come to pass that there shall come peoples, and the inhabitants of many cities; and the inhabitants of one city shall go to another, saying, Let us go speedily to pray before the LORD, and to seek the LORD of hosts; I will go also. Yes, many peoples and strong nations shall come to seek the LORD of hosts in Jerusalem, and to pray before the LORD. Thus says the LORD of hosts: In those days it shall come to pass that ten men shall take hold out of all languages of the nations, even shall take hold of the skirt of him that is a Jew, saying, "We will go with you; for we have heard that God is with you." (Zech. 8:20–23)

This prophetic passage fits in precisely with what the Lord said in Matthew while speaking to His disciples concerning the last days. He said, ". . . this gospel of the kingdom shall be preached in all the world for a witness unto all nations; and then shall the end come" (Matt. 24:14). One would expect the gospel of the kingdom to be preached during the kingdom period. The Lord will be seated on the throne, and His kingdom authority will reach all parts of the earth. The Church will rule with Him and be His representatives to all parts of the earth that are occupied by humans. The gospel of the kingdom is given in great detail in Matthew's Gospel 5–7. It is far different than the gospel of salvation that is preached in the sixth dispensation, which is this present or Church Age.

The Close of the Dispensation

The seventh dispensation closes with a great calamity as God takes a personal hand in judgment upon those who rebel against Him. The earth and mankind have just experienced a 1000 year period of unprecedented peace, righteousness, blessing, and prosperity, with Jesus seated as king on the throne of authority. There can be little excuse for rebellious men; for not only do they have the Lord on earth with them, but they are also surrounded by the resurrected saints who witness to the possibility of righteousness and of godly living.

After this lengthy time in which Satan has been bound and his activity restricted by God, he is once again set free to carry out his nefarious schemes. He quickly presents a plan and a program that is in opposition to God and multitudes of men promptly accept him as leader and flock to his standard. The natural man feels he has been restrained

The Seventh Dispensation: The Millennial Kingdom

and not allowed to do or express his own will, so any alternate plan is welcomed.

This study has already shown the weakness and the error of the man who thinks he has to follow his own conscience. The wise man in Proverbs said,

> There is a way that seems right unto a man, but the end thereof are the ways of death. (Prov. 14:12)

This last of the dispensations reveals the final proof that, apart from the character of God Himself, there is no righteousness that man can attain or gain by his own efforts. Fallen man is at enmity with God and he is completely, totally, and hopelessly lost—estranged from God and unable to do a thing to better his condition. The Bible says, "The heart is deceitful above all things, and desperately wicked; who can know it?" (Jer. 17:9). The best way to show the tragedy of the close of God's plan for the ages is to quote from the Bible the final judgment that occurs because of man's failure:

> And when the thousand years are ended, Satan shall be loosed out of his prison, and shall go out to deceive the nations which are in the four quarters of the earth, Gog and Magog, togather them together to battle; the number of whom is as the sand of the sea. And they went up on the breadth of the earth, and compassed the camp of the saints about, and the beloved city; and fire came down from God out of heaven, and devoured them. (Rev. 20:7–9)

Following the seventh dispensation, in which the gospel of the kingdom will be preached to all the world, the

Scripture just quoted adds these meaningful words: "And then shall the end come." What end is being spoken of? Is it speaking of the end of the world? The end of the human race? The end of creation? Oblivion? The biblical answer to that question is: the end of time as men know and live in it. The end that is being brought to the fore by the Lord for man's perusal includes the end of sin, the end of Satan's career, and the end of man's rebellion against God. More importantly, in the light of this study, it will bring to an end the long series of tests for righteousness that God has conducted with men down through the ages.

Conclusion

At this juncture, the experiment of God with men, with the ages, and with righteousness has been completed. God has set the standard for righteousness. Apart from the righteousness of God Himself, all else falls far short of His standard. God has proven beyond all question that man, without the imputed righteousness that is found in Christ, is unable to produce anything that is acceptable to deity.

With the completion of God's plan for the ages, what men have known as *time* has come to an abrupt end. What has become true of time has also become true of the human race, as far as reproduction is concerned. All creation has entered the condition of eternity. There is no further need of reproduction to ensure the continuity of the race. According to Revelation 22, all men will be in a fixed, unchangeable state—the righteous are fixed in righteousness, and the filthy are fixed in the state they are in.

Satan's career as a free-roving agent of evil has been brought to an end as he is confined to the lake of fire. Sin has been dealt with, paid for, and removed as a threat to

God's Plan for the Ages

any creature; never again to enslave or mar the handiwork of God. All is well in God's creation.

Postscript

Having come to the end of God's plan for the ages, the view now turns to that of future eternity. Many Christians believe they will spend all future eternity in a far distant place called heaven, a place of pure bliss. This belief is in error, for the Scriptures teach man will live and be blessed here on earth. True, it will be a new and quite different earth; but nevertheless, it will be earth and the home God intended for man. Man was created as a terrestrial being, and every part of the physical makeup of man is designed for life on earth. God's intent from the beginning was for the earth to be the home of man, and His intent has never changed. The wonder of it all will be that God is the one who will change residence—not man.

> And I heard a great voice out of heaven saying, Behold, the tabernacle of God is with men, and he will dwell with them, and they shall be his people, and God himself shall be with them, and be their God. (Rev. 21:3)

Imagine! God dwelling among men and fellowshipping with them here on earth. Incredible!

To order additional copies of

God's Plan for the Ages

send $11.95 plus $3.95 shipping and handling to:

Books, Etc.
PO Box 1406
Mukilteo, WA 98275

or have your credit card ready and call:

(800) 917-BOOK